PRAISE FOR
TODAY'S WONDER WOMEN

"As a young girl, it was my imagination that led me to become one of the first leading female live action superheroes of color. The key to playing a superhero is belief. In these pages, Asha has captured a glimpse of real-life superheroes. Women who not only possess the ability to believe but a superpower to inspire."

—**Ciera Foster**, actress, Livewire in *Ninjak vs. the Valiant Universe*

"This collection of stories, essays, and interviews celebrates a diverse set of inspiring women across the globe who are leveling the playing field for future generations of women and girls. Any reader will find wisdom, experiences, and lessons that resonate with them in the pages of this book. This is a must-read for gender justice advocates everywhere working to secure gender equity in their communities and workplaces."

—**Emerald Archer, PhD**, director, Center for the Advancement of Women, Mount Saint Mary's University, Los Angeles

"A beautiful cross-section of inspiration and leadership, offering more than platitudes or stories of luck or happenstance. *Today's Wonder Women* is full of ideas and organizations to help you further pursue what you were born to do."

—**Kristie Holmes**, cochair, United Nations Civil Society Press and Media Subcommittee

"*Today's Wonder Women* is more than inspiring stories of epic culture-shifting leaders. It's a guide for realizing our time is now, our power is within, and the change is us. Asha Dahya provides a must-read resource for anyone ready to forge a living legacy through grit, vision, humanity, and audacious belief in their own ability to affect change."

—**Joy Donnell**, author, *Beyond Brand*

"*Today's Wonder Women* gives women the opportunity to experience people just like them doing extraordinary work that impacts the world in a powerful and positive way. Asha's inclusion of individuals from different walks of life and career paths makes this an easy-to-engage book for anyone looking for great inspiration."

—**Sabrina K. Garba**, founder, Women's Impact Accelerator and
Glass Ladder Group

"Asha Dahya delivers hope. The women chronicled here, from activists to entrepreneurs, will provide every feminist in your life not only with inspiration but with motivation to go out and change the world."

—**Jennifer Wright**, author, *We Came First: Dating Advice from
Women in History*

"There are moments in history when we remember who we are, we begin to challenge ideals that no longer work for us and we set out to create an entirely new framework of womanhood that includes all of us—women, women of color, mothers, all who feel underrepresented and overlooked. We are at that moment right now. In *Today's Wonder Women*, Asha Dahya gives voice to those who we all need to hear today on our journey toward change—women who turned adversity into strength to help others, women who defied all odds, women who stand up and lead every day and forge a new path forward. These stories will resonate with many women across the globe and all who need to hear—we can do it."

—**Simona Grace**, founder, Moms in Office PAC

TODAY'S WONDER WOMEN

Everyday Superheroes
Who Are Changing the World

ASHA DAHYA

ixia
PRESS

Mineola, New York

Bibliographical Note

Today's Wonder Women: Everyday Superheroes Who Are Changing the World
is a new work, first published by Ixia Press in 2020.

International Standard Book Number

ISBN-13: 978-0-486-83928-8
ISBN-10: 0-486-83928-1

Ixia Press
An imprint of Dover Publications, Inc.

Manufactured in the United States by LSC Communications
83928101

www.doverpublications.com/ixiapress

2 4 6 8 10 9 7 5 3 1

2020

CONTENTS

INTRODUCTION

IF SOMEONE HAD TOLD ME WHEN I WAS ELEVEN THAT one day I would write and publish a book about inspiring, badass women from around the world, based on an interview series I started on a blog that I launched as a hobby, I would've either laughed or been very confused. Eleven was the age I first started dreaming about my future and decided very adamantly that I was going to become an actress and move to Hollywood from my home in Australia, where I grew up. While I did end up working in the entertainment industry, and sure enough moved to Los Angeles in 2008, it was not to become a big-screen star.

After studying film and journalism at university in Australia, I basically fell into the TV hosting world at the age of twenty and have never really looked back. Starting out hosting a national daily kids' variety show in Brisbane, Australia, I eventually moved to Sydney and then Los Angeles, working for a number of globally recognized platforms, brands, and networks: Disney, ABC, Nickelodeon, Myspace, MSN, Fox, MTV, Sony, and more. For a solid decade I mastered the art of entertainment, pop culture, and lifestyle hosting and producing. I was going to industry parties, earning great money, and living in a big city where I felt like I was on top of the world. I thought I was set in my career, until I started to become disillusioned and bored. I wanted more out of life and my work but had no idea what that looked like.

At the same time, my personal life was not exactly where I imagined it would be. I was married at the age of twenty-four to a man from my church in Los Angeles, where things quickly went south for a number of reasons. That in turn affected my career trajectory. At the age of twenty-nine I decided to divorce him. It was a decision I never thought I would have to make. I'm quite sure no one ever does. I was lucky to get away without any major hurdles, except the emotional ones, of course.

Going through a divorce in my late twenties, leaving my large church community (which had basically become my de facto family, as I was so far away from my biological one), and having to start all over again was the worst time of my life, but I can look back now and tell you it turned out to be the best.

I moved to a different part of the city; I made new friends, the majority of which were female filmmakers, producers, writers, content creators, actors, and feminists. I was craving a community of women and wanted to hear their stories, especially those who had experienced major setbacks of difficult struggles like I had, so that I would feel less alone in my pain. It felt as if my divorce was forcing me to find a whole new community. I started unlearning all that I was told to mold myself into, through culture, religion, and gender expectations, and constructing myself from scratch, which for the first time felt authentic and raw. I became drawn to other women who I could see were unapologetically living their own authentic lives, despite backlash from others.

While I was going through my divorce I took a trip back to Australia to spend time with my parents and figure out what I was going to do with my life, and I happened to find an old folder of newspaper and magazine clippings I had been keeping since I was in high school. The folder was filled with stories and articles about women, the majority of them noncelebrities and everyday women and girls, who were doing some incredible and inspiring things around the world. These were op-eds that were found in popular women's magazines, and yet at the time, although I was obsessed with the idea of conquering Hollywood, it became clear that a seed was planted deep inside me about the power of ordinary heroic women who were changing the world. I was taken aback. It was as if I was rediscovering my first love all over again. I remember flying back to Los Angeles with a renewed sense of purpose and mission for my life. I started a little blog in 2012 as a hobby, called GirlTalkHQ.com. I wanted to share other women's stories about real life, as a kind of "digital" support community through media content. Over time, as the blog grew and I refined what the main focus of its content was, I realized I was doing what I was always meant to be doing—being a voice and offering a platform to amplify the voices of other women who were looking for a way to share their stories.

All of a sudden I stopped caring about the superficial ambitions I had for myself and found true meaning in this endeavor. Which brings me to this book, *Today's Wonder Women*. This is a book I believe I needed to write for myself, for my younger as well as future self, and I am so honored I can now share it with the world. This book is not about me; it is a reminder to the world that although we may be enamored with the shiny, glittery, and loud things that compete for our focus, authentic and heroic women, girls, and female-identifying individuals are all around us and deserve our attention. Writing this book has been one of the most therapeutic, healing, and joy-inducing experiences of my life. While my daily news feed would instantly flood my mind with negative thoughts, the knowledge that there are powerful individuals who are creating change every day made me smile at the thought of being privileged enough to share their stories with the world.

I have my mother, Kamini, to thank for much of my deep-seated passion. Although she never pushed anything on me, I vividly remember growing up hearing about her love for independent Indian films that were based on stories of heroic Indian and South Asian women who defied social taboos and customs for the sake of doing what was right. It was the earliest introduction to feminism I can remember, without it ever having really been labeled as such. My own mother, who migrated from East Africa to the UK and Australia, had three children, got her master's degree in teaching at the age of fifty, started a whole new career at fifty-plus, and taught me through her own life about values such as loyalty, compassion, curiosity, and a love for community.

I hope that as you immerse yourselves in the stories in these pages, they will serve as a tool of encouragement and empowerment for you to find your own seed of passion (if you haven't yet!) and be a reminder that heroes don't necessarily wear capes and have fictional superpowers, although as a film nerd I am totally all about cheering on the badass women on the big screen! A hero is someone you find in your community, in your workplace, in your place of worship, in your networking group, in your place of study, and even in your home. You can even be the hero of your own story. When we show up in the world as our true, authentic selves, I believe that is when the magic starts to happen and lives begin to change.

WOMEN IN
LEADERSHIP

GROWING UP I NEVER QUESTIONED THE DEFAULT IMAGE of a leader being male. Whether in church, in the political footage I saw on TV, in every school I attended, or even in the media companies I started working for as a young adult, the closer you got to the top, the more male (and white) it became. Being able to question and examine this disparity now as a woman and a mom of two is an integral part of my passion for gender equality at every level. The statistics show we need to encourage leadership among more young women and minorities if we ever hope to truly see change.

In mid-2019 the Fortune 500 list showed a significant improvement in the number of women in the CEO role. Thirty-three of the highest grossing companies listed are being led by women for the first time ever. While the total percentage is only 6.6 percent showing we still need to see more progress in terms of gender equality in leadership, the current numbers show things are changing slowly.

When women make up just over 5 percent of the world's largest corporations' CEOs, what kind of message does this send to women and girls everywhere about their own abilities to lead?

As Marian Wright Edelman, founder of the Children's Defense Fund, once famously said, "You can't be what you can't see," which is why I am profiling the lives and work of ordinary, heroic women who have pushed past systemic barriers and their own personal struggles to attain leadership positions that are impacting the world in powerful ways.

KAYLA NGUYEN

KAYLA NGUYEN HAS A STORY THAT WILL RESONATE WITH MANY WOMEN ACROSS AMERICA TODAY. SHE IS AN IMMIGRANT WITH A PASSION FOR SCIENCE, WHO OVERCAME A DISABILITY TO WIN THE PRESTIGIOUS LEMELSON-MIT STUDENT PRIZE IN 2018. AS AMERICA BATTLES OVER POLICIES RELATING TO IMMIGRATION, KAYLA'S JOURNEY IS PROOF TO YOUNG WOMEN ESPECIALLY THAT YOU CAN ACHIEVE ANYTHING DESPITE THE ODDS. AS AN IMMIGRANT AND WOMAN OF COLOR MYSELF WHO HAS HAD TO BATTLE MISCONCEPTIONS ABOUT WHO I AM, I KNOW STORIES LIKE THIS ARE GOING TO CHANGE THE WORLD. PLEASE ENJOY KAYLA'S STORY, IN HER OWN WORDS.

I BELIEVE IN ORDER FOR YOUNG GIRLS AND WOMEN TO learn about the power of facing failure with resilience, people must use their success as a platform to expose not only their accomplishments, but also their challenges. I have noticed that many scientists choose to only acknowledge the highlights of their scientific careers, rather than their entire journey. Of course there are struggles, but what a general audience sees are the end results: the Nobel Prize, the MacArthur genius award, etc. These awards are a great honor; however, they do not teach young scientists that they will face challenges and failures on their path to success. I want to start off by sharing who I am and what I have struggled with before I share my work as a scientist and inventor.

Before I was born, my grandfather was a Vietnamese Air Force general who helped the United States during the Vietnam War. Because of this, he was a prisoner of war for seventeen years in a re-education camp. I was born while he was gone, in Gia Dinh Province in Ho Chi Minh City, Vietnam. Once he was released in 1992, my family and I gained political asylum and migrated to America in 1993.

My childhood was pretty difficult. As an immigrant family living in the US, we struggled with social, economic, and language barriers. My weekends consisted of either helping my mother clean laundry rooms of apartment complexes or collecting cans from garbage bins with my grandmother to make revenue from recyclables.

Even though my family worked full-time, low-wage jobs, the pursuit of education was always of the utmost importance to them. So in addition to working and raising me, my mother attended community college. My mother graduated with a BS in biochemistry from California State University, Fullerton in 2002 at the age of forty. She is the reason I understand the value of hard work. Obstacles and failures never led to her abandoning the things she cared about: providing for her family, raising me, and continuing her education. Because of her, I have never felt "turned away" by failure.

As a student, my grades were always a bit polarizing. Subjects like math and physics came naturally to me, but history and Latin were time-consuming and extremely difficult. I was never good at spelling or multiple-choice exams and as a result, I never did well in those classes. As a high school student, I got Cs and Ds in history and Latin, grades that would be appalling to the regular PhD students in physics, chemistry, or any type of science.

However, I did know what I was good at, and that was building stuff. As a kid, I would build skateboards or simple experimental contraptions like a mini tornado inside of a Coke bottle. These experiences helped build my passion for invention.

I decided to major in physics and attend the University of California, Santa Barbara (UCSB), where I was part of a special program called the College of Creative Studies. Here, exams were oral and based on important physical concepts. For my undergrad research project, I built an electrostatic force microscopy set-up that could image the surface charges of organic photovoltaics [the branch of technology concerned with the production of electric current at the junction of two substances] under laser illumination, further extending my passion for invention.

After I graduated from UCSB, I came to Cornell University to pursue my PhD under Professor David Muller. I struggled a lot when I first started. I had difficulty recognizing the differences between letters, shapes, and objects and completing timed exams. These weaknesses made it challenging for me to perform at the level the PhD program required and, in effect, I did not perform as well as my peers.

Professor Muller noticed that although I understood the material and the physics extremely well, I still had problems differentiating between letters, shapes, and objects. By his suggestions and support, I tested for ADHD. I instead found out that I had a vision processing disorder. I knew that I always had issues disentangling similar visualizations, but I thought that if I worked hard enough, was careful enough, or found alternative methods of studying, I could overcome these barriers.

In addition, even after my diagnosis of my visual impairment, my family and friends told me that what I had was normal. They emphasized that everyone struggles with some sort of visualization problem, whether it was right-left-handedness or shapes and objects. They told me that I did not have a learning disability because I would not have gotten into a PhD program otherwise. This lack of support and acknowledgment of my diagnosis made it difficult for me to accept and feel comfortable with it.

Even worse, although I could understand why certain things would take me twice as long to accomplish in comparison to other students, I was still embarrassed by my challenges—so much so, that I ended up not vocalizing my disability to the other professors and staff in the department. Instead of asking for help, I continued with my struggles; this became the biggest regret of my life.

Over time, I realized that if I talk about my struggles with vision processing disorder, it can let other young people with learning disabilities know that they are not alone and that they should not feel ashamed.

> I HOPE MY STORY AS A CHILD WITH A LEARNING IMPAIRMENT, WHO GREW UP IN A PREDOMINANTLY IMMIGRANT COMMUNITY, CAN INSPIRE PEOPLE NOT TO GIVE UP ON THEIR DREAMS AND GOALS NO MATTER WHAT LIFE GIVES THEM.

Graduate school requires an immense amount of work and mental prowess. I knew my vision processing disorder would make achieving success more challenging, but I told myself I could not give up. Through hard work and dedication, a group of amazing scientists and I coinvented the electron microscope pixel array detector (EMPAD)—an electron diffraction detector.

The EMPAD enables us to observe what happens inside computer chips, proteins important to Alzheimer's disease, or nanocomposite in paintings like *The Scream* by Edvard Munch. The EMPAD accomplishes these tasks by extracting structural, optical, chemical, electronic, and magnetic properties from atoms. This same data could also be used to create faster computers, cheaper electric cars, and better biological scoping/treatment, art conservation, and drugs that we design to cure diseases.

I hope my story as a child with a learning impairment, who grew up in a predominantly immigrant community, can inspire people not to give up on their dreams and goals no matter what life gives them. My perseverance has led to many amazing opportunities, including receiving the Lemelson-MIT Student Prize award and licensing EMPAD to ThermoFisher Scientific, which enabled it to be sold around the world. I was lucky enough to travel to Vienna, Austria, to give a TEDxVienna talk about EMPAD.

So much of my success has been made possible because of the incredible support I received from professors and mentors throughout my journey. They taught me that learning comes in different forms and every brain is wired to retain information in its own way. Without their efforts to accommodate for my learning needs, I could not have finished my PhD or become a scientist. Ultimately, my hope is that both my research and personal story can help and inspire people everywhere.

JACKIE LOMAX

WOMEN MAKE UP HALF THE WORKFORCE IN THE UNITED States today but represent only 24 percent of STEM (Science, Technology, Engineering, Math) careers. *CNN Money* reports that STEM jobs are growing at 1.7 times the rate of non-STEM jobs, and the US is simply not producing enough candidates to fill them.

Experts say there is a decline in women graduating from college with computing degrees, and they believe the interest in all STEM jobs must start as young as possible, in kindergarten even. There is a concerted effort to engage young girls in STEM initiatives, but where there needs to be particular focus in the drive to engage women and girls is among minorities. They already have less access to initiatives, which makes minorities sorely underrepresented in STEM. Of all engineers, only 14 percent are women, and 5 percent are African American. One of the solutions, says Brittney Grimes at Stemjobs.com, is to engage minority children (which includes racial minorities as well as those from a lower socioeconomic situation) in programs specifically geared toward them, in an attempt to even the playing field.

One woman who is certainly doing this in her community is entrepreneur and mother Jackie Lomax. Based out of Chicago, Jackie is the founder of Girls 4 Science, a nonprofit organization that addresses the lack of accessible quality science programs for female youth ages ten to eighteen in the Chicago area. She believes science exposure and increased scientific literacy will equip young women

to confidently pursue STEM studies and careers.

Tell me about your daughter; where did her love of science come from?

My daughter has always loved science. As a child I witnessed her curiosity in terms of the questions that she would ask me, where, in most cases, those questions usually ended with more questions. I began to notice, through my daughter and her friends, that she was not the only girl looking for an outlet to explore science. As a parent I felt it was my responsibility to take her and other girls' scientific ambition to a whole new level.

Girls 4 Science exists in order to open new doors for young Chicago women who have been discouraged from fields because they have not been given the opportunity to learn. I have neither the background nor the training to give my daughter the answers to science questions. Instead, I established an organization with the assistance of talented industry trailblazers and like-minded thinkers who volunteer their time to share their knowledge with our girls.

Tell me about your career background and your experience with STEM industries.

My background is in business and journalism. After discovering the lack of opportunities for my daughter to participate in STEM, I was exposed to many new ideas about how important this field really is. My experience with STEM is number one, being a consumer, and number two, showing my family its practical daily use in all aspects of their lives.

What steps did you take to create Girls 4 Science and the six-week course?

The Girls 4 Science six-week quarterly modules came about by surveying female Chicago students about their interests in STEM fields and science as a whole. From the results, a group of volunteers worked to create themed laboratory sessions and field trips. In our current program, volunteer mentors assist with facilitating the program and act as subject matter experts.

Since 2009 you have seen more than five hundred girls come through your program. How does this make you feel?

When I look back at how far the program has come and watch our girls turn into tomorrow's leaders, I feel a great sense of pride. The pride is in the participants and the mentors who make Girls 4 Science an influential part of breaking down gender stereotypes in the field. Most girls who enter into our program decide to major in STEM-related fields in college, and find a career path in a field that was or is primarily male-dominated. Girls 4 Science as a whole means more than just a STEM education; it means positive influences to show that girls can do anything they set their mind to.

There is a huge focus on getting girls interested in STEM, with organizations like yours as well as Girls Who Code and Black Girls Code, for example. What impact do you foresee this having on the next generation of STEM workforce participants?

I think this impact has a great chance to "reverse the curse" by including more diverse talent in STEM fields. The economy will be more robust with improved earning potential for families. Girls 4 Science aims to introduce new ideas to females who have the potential to become leaders in the workplace. Every day, in the field of science, we are making progress in physics, engineering, medicine, technology, and countless other disciplines. My primary focus has been the advancement of women in these disciplines. The reason Girls 4 Science exists is to introduce science to those young women who don't have the opportunity to explore science in the traditional high school experiences.

THE PRIDE IS IN THE PARTICIPANTS AND THE MENTORS WHO MAKE GIRLS 4 SCIENCE AN INFLUENTIAL PART OF BREAKING DOWN GENDER STEREOTYPES IN THE FIELD.

What advice would you give to other parents who are struggling to get their girls interested in STEM subjects?

Parents should expose their children to positive mentors who can guide them during their careers to have a successful future. Girls 4 Science strongly encourages parent participation and we work to engage them as volunteers in our Saturday Science Academy. At home, I recommend parents talk to their daughters and at the same time engage in home science projects that both parent and child can work on. Talk with mentors to discover ways you can be involved as a parent, whether it is taking your child to a museum or reading a certain book together.

Who are your STEM role models?

My personal STEM role model is Linda McGill Boasmond, the first female African American to own and operate her own chemical manufacturing plant, Chicago-based Cedar Concepts Corporation. Finding women who are breaking down barriers is inspiring motivation for a program like Girls 4 Science. Linda, a supporter of the program, has shown young women that determination and belief in yourself are the keys to future success.

GLORIA FELDT

SHE HAS BEEN CALLED THE "VOICE OF EXPERIENCE" by *People* magazine, as well as garnering other accolades such as *Glamour*'s "Woman of the Year" and one of *Vanity Fair*'s "America's Top 200 Women Leaders, Legends, and Trailblazers." When you are carrying around credentials like that, you know your voice is important and impactful.

Gloria Feldt has spent her lifetime using her platform to advocate for women and girls in leadership positions and understands the intrinsic value they bring to the decision-making table, no matter where they are.

Hailing from rural Texas, the best-selling author and speaker ended up dropping out of high school and became pregnant as a teen. By the time she was twenty she had three kids with her high school sweetheart, but that was far from the end of her story. Fast forward a number of years, Gloria became the President and CEO of Planned Parenthood Federation of America from 1996 to 2006.

Since leaving the health care provider, Gloria has taken her advocacy to the next level. She has authored four books and regularly speaks at events about the need for more women in leadership roles. She currently travels the country with her Take The Lead organization, which is about tapping into the current wave of female empowerment and helping women embrace their own power in an age where there is a need for feminine leadership.

Gloria believes we are living in a moment where women are fighting for equality more than ever. She has been fighting against antichoice lawmakers for many years and is now taking that experience into a much wider landscape for many more women to benefit from.

Why is encouraging female leadership important to you?

I grew up in a time and place when women were not given aspirations for careers or opportunities to share in life's accomplishments or wealth. Women's equality in all areas has always been about simple justice to me. And now we know businesses do better (are more profitable) and the world would be a safer and healthier place for everyone if there were greater gender parity in leadership.

What was your first leadership position that propelled your career initially?

Having three children by the time I was twenty. You learn many leadership skills from that experience! I was serendipitously recruited for and offered my first CEO position after teaching at Head Start for five years. I had always wanted to be a teacher. I accepted the position as executive director of the small new Planned Parenthood affiliate in West Texas, thinking I'd do it for three years and then go back to teaching. Thirty years later I retired as the organization's national president. So you never know where life will give you the opportunity to lead.

Talk to us about being a teen mom, a high school dropout from rural Texas, and how you defied all expectations despite your situation.

I felt very weak and powerless at the time, and although I was married, I felt isolated in a new city with few friends or family. But I had always been a good student. So I continued my education, first through a high school correspondence course and then taking twelve years to get my college degree. Learning was one thing I knew I did have the ability to do, and that achievement helped me to tackle others.

IF YOU KEEP FIGHTING THE SAME BATTLE OVER AND OVER AGAIN AND GETTING THE SAME RESULT, THAT'S A SURE SIGN YOU NEED TO CHANGE YOUR STRATEGY.

Before becoming a best-selling author and entrepreneur, you were the CEO of Planned Parenthood Federation of America. Why are reproductive rights so important to you?

I knew how hard it was to be a very young mother. The birth control pill saved my life when it became available. As I became more attuned to women's rights, or the lack of them, I realized that to be fully free and to be an equal citizen, everyone needs two things: First is to own and control your own body. Second is to have a means to support yourself financially. If you have those two things, then you can be whatever you want to be. And you can contribute your best self to the world.

When you look at the current political landscape of women's health care, what encouragement and important advice would you give to women who are looking to fight back against regressive ideas and policies?

The same advice I've always given. Stop fighting *back*. Focus on fighting *forward*. Set the agenda. And understand you're not just fighting for health care, you're fighting for women's fundamental human and civil rights.

How are you looking to change the dynamics holding women back from their potential with "Take The Lead"?

If you keep fighting the same battle over and over again and getting the same result, that's a sure sign you need to change your strategy. Aiming for power sharing by advancing gender parity in leadership is that new strategy that I think is the most effective one now. I was shocked to find when researching my latest book, *No Excuses: 9 Ways Women Can Change How We Think About Power*, that women's own culturally learned ambivalence toward power has been holding us back from achieving parity.

Though the second wave of the feminist movement opened the doors and changed certain discriminatory laws, women have been stuck at under 20 percent of the top leadership positions across all sectors of the economy. I decided I had to change that and I developed our "9 Leadership Power Tools to Accelerate Your Career" program. It gives women amazing breakthroughs so they can embrace their power with authenticity, intention, confidence, and joy.

How can women in positions of leadership become agents for change in their lives and communities?

The most important thing a woman in a position of leadership can do is to nurture, mentor, and sponsor other women into leadership— to teach women to create a new paradigm for how we think about power. The male model has been a belief that resources are always finite, that there is a pie and if I take a slice of it, there's less for you. In truth, if I help you and you help me, we both can create more of everything: more wealth, more innovation, more pie all around!

What makes you a powerful woman?

They say you write the book you need to read. I'm still learning to own my power. I intentionally try to choose power over fear every day. Even though that's not how I was socialized to be and it remains a challenge, I set daily intentions. Often I don't succeed in achieving them all, but I learn from each setback.

DOROTHY GIBBONS

MANY OF US KNOW SOMEONE WHOSE LIFE HAS BEEN affected by breast cancer. Some of us may have gone through it ourselves. In the United States, breast cancer is the most common cancer among women, where one in eight (12 percent) will develop invasive breast cancer during their lifetime. The American Cancer Society estimates more than 240,000 women will be diagnosed, and over forty thousand will die from it. Breast cancer is the second-leading cause of cancer death in women, affecting one in thirty-six (3 percent) of those diagnosed.

There is some good news, however. Since 1989, death rates from breast cancer have been dropping (although slightly increased among African American women), with larger decreases in women younger than fifty. These are believed to be the result of finding breast cancer earlier through screening and increased awareness, as well as better treatments.

Which brings us to why clinics like The Rose in Texas, and women like Dorothy Gibbons, are important in the world of breast health. Because the US health care system is still so fragmented and complex in a number of ways, many women aren't able to get the preventative and early care they need to survive or even detect signs of breast cancer. The Rose has become a pivotal tool, especially for low-income and migrant women in parts of Texas. Dorothy is one of the original founders, who has documented her decades-long work in a new book, appropriately titled *The Women of The Rose*.

Dorothy Gibbons (center, holding scissors) with the Rose staff

In your book about The Rose clinic, you walk the reader through decades of growing an idea to help women in Texas get the right resources to prevent, diagnose, and treat breast cancer. Why did you want to share your journey?

The Rose never would have made it without people believing in us. I wanted to show what it's like to run a nonprofit; demonstrate that a nonprofit is a business like any other business and requires the same gutsy entrepreneurial leadership spirit as any business owner, doing whatever it takes to stay alive and get through the day.

I hope my story will encourage anyone who has a dream to do something better to at least try, and in the trying, discover their own passions. It's all worth it.

What do you want people to know about the importance of ensuring everyone has the coverage they need, no matter their ZIP code or socioeconomic status?

I doubt I could begin to explain all the issues involved or the tragedies that await when we continue to live under a broken health care system. A Canadian physician once told me that his country had two systems: Public health and Private Pay health. But our country has three: Public, Private, and "No have" system.

I believe the worst prejudice we face in this country is the prejudice to poverty. While having insurance coverage doesn't equate to "good health," it sure helps. We would need to address what "access" really means and include having adequate physician coverage and communication, being able to navigate the maze of traditional health care, being able to find the right treatment in the community one lives in, pharmaceuticals that actually work, incorporating complementary medicine, and allowing the individual's belief system to be part of the healing.

Years ago, I remember being appalled at hearing someone say that a person's chance at surviving a disease like breast cancer depends on how good their insurance is and how much money they have in the bank. After witnessing firsthand all the compromises a poor or uninsured person has to make, I've come to see the truth in that statement. There has to be a better way.

You have shared about your faith as well as your feminism. How do these two topics factor into the work you do today?

Feminism provides the passion, faith provides the belief, and together they create a backbone that everything else hangs from. I see those topics reflected in the work my leadership team completed when we reviewed and updated our values. Sixteen women came together for six months to hammer out what The Rose stood for and what values they as our leadership team embraced.

Their top five values were Integrity and Honesty, Spirituality, Family, Dependability, and Teamwork. I was so proud to see how they would be integrated and reflected in our daily work. While I understand most corporations would question having "family" as a value, my team was clear in how it would be held up at The Rose.

I'm a big believer in electing women, as there are a whole load of bad health policies being pushed by male politicians who don't understand women's health care. What are your thoughts on this?

I agree we need more women in politics, although after watching the 2016 presidential election and the total lack of civility, I sincerely question why any sane woman would agree to put herself in that arena! But they do, and thank God they do. I deeply believe that the feminine in each of us, male or female, needs to be valued.

The feminine in each of us knows how to nourish, to take care of self and others, and she also knows how to fiercely protect those she loves. Imagine this world, and the future, if the feminine were allowed to fully exist.

> FEMINISM PROVIDES THE PASSION, FAITH PROVIDES THE BELIEF, AND TOGETHER THEY CREATE A BACKBONE THAT EVERYTHING ELSE HANGS FROM.

Can you explain why it is important to also donate to organizations like The Rose who are helping women who have been diagnosed?

Early detection is still the best chance a woman has for beating this disease and having a chance at survival. The fact that we've built a culture where women are encouraged to care for themselves and one in which every woman who has a mammogram with us helps an uninsured woman receive the same quality service, is part of why it is so important that The Rose continue. Our hallmark program and incredibly important service is Patient Navigation. The woman who is uninsured and can't afford the $150 for a mammogram sure doesn't have the money to pay the $150,000 (or more) for treatment. Our Navigators move every uninsured woman who is diagnosed into treatment and walk with them on their journey.

Can you share some of the most impactful feedback from women you have helped that has stuck with you throughout the years?

"Women can handle anything including a diagnosis of breast cancer, just don't make us wait for answers or be condescending to us."

"Having an 'option' is the most important factor in life."

"I wasn't treated as a poor person and never felt like I was in a clinic having to beg for service."

"The Rose gave me 'back' my dignity."

KEDMA OUGH

THERE IS A SAYING: "NOT ALL SUPERHEROES WEAR CAPES," and while that is certainly the truth, as it turns out some actually DO wear one. Kedma Ough is a leader in the business world, a mentor to entrepreneurs, and specifically a champion of women and minorities looking to start their own businesses in a landscape that is still very heavily male-dominated. She is also a powerful speaker, giving keynote addresses at conferences where she appears onstage wearing an actual cape. Kedma's personal story of escaping an abusive family member, staying in hiding for a number of years in fear of being retaliated against, and eventually using an educational scholarship as the opportunity for a path to a better life is nothing short of inspiring. When she stands onstage in that cape, she doesn't just bring her MBA knowledge and decades of business expertise to her audience, she brings her whole self and talks about why the idea of waiting around for the proverbial superhero may not be the key to a happy and successful life. For her, it was the realization that SHE had to be the hero in her own story, and this is the foundational idea in the work she does to help aspiring entrepreneurs today.

You are an award-winning thought leader, business development expert, and champion of entrepreneurs. Where did you get your start professionally?

I was hired as the SBA Women's Business Center Director in Tucson, Arizona, where my job was to help socially and economically disadvantaged women succeed in business. Immediately I knew it was my calling and I have now been in the economic development/business development industry for more than twenty years.

One of my favorite things about you is how adamant you are about empowering people to be their own superhero. Can you tell me about the path and the incidents that led you to realizing this?

I think as children we are taught by society that people can and will save us when we are in distress, but unfortunately that is not the case for many children. I was one of those children. I grew up in a very difficult home environment and I realized that no matter how many times I prayed or wished for someone to come rescue me that no one showed up at my doorstep and rescued me. So I learned at a very young age that I had control over one thing—my mind. The ability to master my thoughts and discipline my mind was the only thing no one could rob from me. When I entered into college my life changed forever. I was attending an evening class at a community college on the East Coast and I received a 911 page from my therapist at the time. I remember running out of the college classroom and into the cold. Frantically I searched for a payphone and dialed her number. She responded, "Kedma, listen to me carefully, he is on the way to the college and he said if he finds you he will kill you—you need to seek safety immediately." She was referring to my real-life villain. This was not the movies and there was no superhero waiting to save me. I remember hanging up and going to the parking lot to look for my car, but it was too late. He was already there pacing back and forth by his car, searching for me. I literally went into shock. A small voice in my head said "run Kedma run," but I couldn't run, so I ducked and went from car to car until I got to my car and quietly opened the door and took my books out and retraced my steps back to the payphone to call the person I was seeing at the time for help.

Over the course of a few days, a group of friends found me my first safe haven. It was a basement apartment and it was infested with cockroaches and ants. That would be my home for the next five years. Another group helped me find my first job and I remember telling Patricia in the interview that I was in hiding, but if they would hire me

I would be one of their best employees. And they did! I also sent a very detailed letter to the financial committee of the college pleading my case to be considered for a hardship grant.

The college, after receiving it, invited me to meet with the financial committee and I remember explaining to them that I lost everything—my home, my family, my identity—and the only thing left to live for is an opportunity for an education. They said they needed to deliberate. In the secretary's office where I waited for their decision, I asked for a piece of paper and pen and I wrote a letter to God.

Even though I saw him as the same God that had never been there all those years, I said to him in the letter that if the college would come back and give me an opportunity then for the REST OF MY LIFE I would use the knowledge I learn to open doors to every person that crosses my path. Two hours later the committee came back and granted me a full scholarship to complete college! That solidified the contract and I have been fulfilling it every single day for the last thirty years. Each time I service it, it is a reminder that I have kept my commitment to God to help open doors and break through barriers for others on the path.

Why do you feel it is important to encourage more people to be their own heroes in life?

There are everyday heroes that need to be recognized as incredible role models. Here are the superheroes in my life:

⬦ The single mother who is raising five kids on her own and helping them each go to college.

- ✧ The single parent who is raising a nonverbal autistic son and doing everything possible to help him have a better life.
- ✧ The woman who developed an amazing product for nursing moms so they wouldn't struggle as she did.

You don't have to be famous to be a superhero. Being a superhero is doing things for others in a consistent fashion that puts you in a position as being seen as a role model.

You are a fifth-generation entrepreneur who comes from a family of immigrants, and today you are passionate about helping marginalized groups to become business owners and maximize their potential. What would you say is the power of embracing our unique identities on our path to success in life?

You should never shy away from your unique identities, as they are a part of your DNA. Embracing your identities gives others insight into your courage, your strength, and your spirit. You humanize business. Here are people in my life today that I am supporting because of their story.

- ✧ The Cuban-born entrepreneur that walked for miles and miles to put a lottery ticket in to come to America. The family won and had to leave everything behind and start from the beginning when they arrived in the United States.
- ✧ The Ethiopian-born entrepreneur that was in a refugee camp and was sent to America to start a new life and became the owner of an Ethiopian restaurant.

Even my own life is enriched with uniqueness. My great-great-grandfather peddled trinkets throughout Ireland operating his own entrepreneurial business. Never apologize for being who you are.

You often give keynote speeches and lectures on entrepreneurship, and you come onstage wearing a literal

> BEING A SUPERHERO IS DOING THINGS FOR OTHERS IN A CONSISTENT FASHION THAT PUTS YOU IN A POSITION AS BEING SEEN AS A ROLE MODEL.

superhero cape! What kind of reception have you gotten from audiences after they see you in your outfit and hear your personal story?

Before they know my story they have very strange reactions. Comments I have heard:

✧ Why is she wearing that silly cape?
✧ Is that a gimmick?
✧ Why is she wearing a Halloween costume?
✧ She seems a bit strange. LOL!

After they hear my story they almost always come up and hug me. Then the comments are very different. Comments are more like:

✧ I love that cape on you!
✧ You are so inspirational!
✧ I want my own cape!
✧ You truly are a superhero!

I purposely don't tell people about my story until I am onstage because it teaches them that first impressions are not always the right ones. Never judge a person by their cape, as you don't know yet why they wear it.

The idea of becoming our own hero can often feel very foreign to women especially, who are socialized from an early age to find happiness and success in others. What advice do you have to break through this mind-set?

I always say that you can be smart, successful, and sexy and still be happy. Why do we have to compromise? Why do we have to dim our light in the world? I have a saying that you have every right to B.R.A.G., which means Bring Repetitive Authentic Greatness, to the world. I teach women to do that so they can showcase their gifts and never hide behind them.

Finally, what makes you a powerful woman?

I am not afraid of standing strong in my values. I am not afraid of challenging the status quo. I am not afraid of coming up against very powerful people that create havoc in the world. I am not afraid of being myself, because everything I do is for the benefit of serving others.

ANA FLORES

MANY OF US ARE FAMILIAR WITH THE TERM "INFLUENCER" today. It describes someone who has created a following on one or more social media platforms and been able to leverage that into a bona fide way to earn a living through sponsorship deals and brand partnerships. Digital influencers are today's version of billboards, and some have even transcended the term to become celebrities in their own right (think popular YouTubers or fashion bloggers). But it is not as easy as social media posts make it out to be. It takes a LOT of hard work learning about the digital marketplace and setting yourself apart from the myriad other influencers who are growing in number every day. One woman who knows the ropes very well is Ana Flores, an entrepreneur who has built up the largest digital network of Latina influencers in the United States. For Ana, the endeavor was as much about empowering her fellow Latina entrepreneurs and influencers financially, as well as showing brands and advertisers that they are missing out on major revenue streams by not engaging the growing Latina digital audience, who these influencers are reaching. Ana has dealt with major setbacks along the way to her success, but through it all she has never lost sight of the fact that the #WeAllGrow Latina Network and annual summit she created is above all else about fostering community. As the global economy changes, it is everyday influencers and leaders like Ana Flores who are part of a new generation that are helping to democratize how money is made and who gets to dictate what success looks like.

Tell me how you created #WeAllGrow Latina Network.

I originally founded the company in 2010 as Latina Bloggers Connect. It was the very first network connecting Latina bloggers with brands years before influencer marketing became recognized as an industry. At the core, my intention was to foster a community of fellow Latina bloggers where we could first and foremost find each other. We needed a way to connect to teach each other what we were individually learning about things like SEO, HTML, design, pitching to brands, contributing with media platforms, growing audiences, etc. Back then there were only a handful of communities for digital creators and none addressing the needs of Latinas directly. We were blogging in Spanish and others in both English and Spanish. In order to keep serving the audiences we had nurtured, we needed to monetize our content. In order to monetize, we needed direct access to brands looking to reach Hispanic audiences and we had to do it in the most professional way.

THE WHOLE COMPANY HAS BEEN BUILT ON SETBACKS!

All of this led to our motto of "When one grows, we all grow." But since there was no one ahead of us treading the path, we had to do it and continuously pass along the learnings, resources, and connections.

Five years later, I decided it was time to host our first conference in Los Angeles, and thus the #WeAllGrow Summit was born. I had made most of my connections by attending and speaking at conferences like BlogHer, Mom 2.0, Alt Summit, and others. Though I was always accepted and respected, I was usually the token Latina or one of a handful there. It definitely served to my advantage because as the token Latina I was receiving many brand and media opportunities. I utilized those connections to open up a space where they could find hundreds of Latina influencers to partner with. The influencers already trusted us because for many we had been the first network to offer them paid opportunities and real online connections. Brands like Neutrogena, Dove, Disney, and YouTube

also trusted us because we had been working on campaigns together for five years.

#WeAllGrow Latina Network is the first and largest network of digital Latina influencers in the United States. But you have worked through some major setbacks along the way to your success. Can you share some of those?

The whole company has been built on setbacks! When I launched in 2010 this was the very first company connecting Latina bloggers and digital creators with brands. We had to educate and convince brands not only of the power of digital media but also of the importance of the Hispanic market and why targeting Latina women and their audiences was important.

The company was always built with the community and the mission at the forefront, so when influencer marketing became an actual industry it was difficult for us to thrive in a highly competitive market that had become transactional and technology-driven. I had to decide that I didn't want to be the CEO of a technology company creating relationships via algorithms and decided the focus would then turn completely to growing our successful events, with the annual #WeAllGrow Summit as the tentpole event.

I don't regret the decision, but it meant having to lose our largest source of revenue, which meant that in 2017 I had to let go of the whole team and came close to filing for bankruptcy. Thanks to the support of many women and men around me and the love from the community, we were able to rebound and within months announced our fourth #WeAllGrow Summit, which sold out in twenty-four hours. This gave us not only the cash but also the validation to keep going. Every year it feels like we're in startup mode and that brings a lot of challenges. The positive is that we've stayed true to our mission and our integrity.

Why is it important for brands to pay attention to the Latina demographic, especially when it comes to buying power?

Budgets for multicultural audiences are less than 10 percent of the overall pie. This is especially tough when you're addressing a community with a purchasing power projected at $1.7 trillion and we're 18 percent of the population and driving more than half of the country's population growth. Yet, media budgets don't reflect that at all. The gatekeepers are still deciding how much value to put to our stories and our visibility. That's why free digital platforms where we can share our stories have been essential for our increased visibility and need to be constantly nurtured. Our mission is to elevate the voices and stories of Latinas via the power of community. The digital landscape has provided a platform for us to be able to tell our stories, share our products, raise our voices, and finally be seen. Traditional media, marketing, and advertising wasn't and still isn't doing a good job at representing us, so we've had to do it ourselves.

What advice would you give to women and girls who have entrepreneurial aspirations but don't know where to begin or feel they don't have money/connections/status, etc.?

That it takes much more resilience, commitment, and inner work than what most Instagram #boss hashtags and feeds are selling us. It's very easy to launch a business online these days, but the hard work behind the feeds is still the same. Make sure that from the get-go you prepare yourself for growth by investing in setting up your business entity and do it with a certified professional that can advise you on the best scenario for your business goals. Understand the financial risks involved for you and your family when you go after loans, lines of credit, and credit cards to finance your business. Learn everything you can about financial planning, so you're set up the moment you get your first big deal or sale. Build a team of people you trust and that are aligned with your vision. But more than anything, follow your intuition. Entrepreneurship involves risk-taking and failing.

Finally, what makes you a powerful woman?

Real power comes from choosing which thoughts to pay attention to and trusting our intuition, not the images others create about and for us. I choose every day to trust my chosen path and be guided by my intuition and that makes me feel powerful.

WOMEN OF
ACTIVISM

WHEN I THINK OF ACTIVISTS, I THINK OF WOMEN FROM around the world and throughout history whose actions have literally changed the lives of those around them and continue to impact the world today. I think of Alicia Garza, Patrisse Cullors, and Opal Tometi, who started the Black Lives Matter movement in 2013 as a response to the acquittal of Trayvon Martin's murderer, George Zimmerman. With chapters all over the globe, and the conversations and actions it has prompted regarding race, this movement is easily the most important movement for racial justice since the Civil Rights movement.

I think of Greta Thunberg, the Swedish teen girl and climate activist who started the worldwide #fridaysforfuture protests where school students are now walking out of their classes on Fridays to demand governments and authorities take drastic action on reducing carbon emissions around the world. Greta's unrelenting message to world leaders has earned her a Nobel Peace Prize nomination, as well as global media recognition, which she is using every ounce of to spread her message.

I think of the Muslim and Christian women of Liberia who came together in unity, putting aside their differences, and embarked on a hunger and sex strike during the reign of then-president Charles Taylor. Organized by social worker Leymah Gbowee, the Women of Liberia Mass Action for Peace mobilized with such effectiveness in their communities it eventually led to the downfall of Taylor and the end of a civil war. These women helped the country elect its first female president,

Ellen Johnson Sirleaf, who was also the first democratically elected female head of state in Africa.

It reminds me of the organizing power of women, their passion for community, and the knowledge that they aren't going to wait around for the proverbial knight in shining armor.

As the South African poet June Jordan famously wrote in her 1980 "Poem for South African Women," which was dedicated to the women and children who put their bodies on the line for a 1956 protest against apartheid, "We are the ones we have been waiting for."

In this chapter you will meet women who embody the spirit of these words in the name of change, not just for themselves but also for others. These everyday superheroes are what it looks like when we rise up to the challenges we see in front of us.

SARA CUNNINGHAM

IF YOU AREN'T FAMILIAR WITH THE ORGANIZATION Free Mom Hugs, I highly encourage you to get to know the founder, Sara Cunningham, whose personal story and abounding amounts of love and boldness are literally transforming the lives of people across this nation.

As the website states, Sara is "a Christian mom with a gay son living in Oklahoma saying enough is enough." For many who have grown up or still live amongst conservative American Christian communities in parts of the Midwest and South, the idea of coming out to their family and friends, or even being affirming in any way of the LGBTQ community, can be difficult and even traumatic.

Sara had to challenge her own perspectives once she learned her son was gay, and her decision to form an activist organization came after learning about the horror stories from the LGBTQ community, which include abandonment from family and even suicide. Free Mom Hugs started in 2016 with a viral Facebook post and has since set the nation on fire by telling the LGBTQ community that they have support no matter what.

I spoke with Sara to learn more about the mission behind Free Mom Hugs.

You are very candid about your personal story struggling with your faith while attending a conservative church and learning that your son was gay. How did you eventually choose to support your son?

Hearing the words, "Mom, I sucked it up for twenty-one years being your son, I need you to suck it up now and be my mom" got my attention. When Parker came out of the closet, I re-examined everything I believed. It took some time but I wanted to get educated on the subject. I also began writing and soon found a private online FB group for moms like me. I realized I was not alone, found faith-based resources, and found my voice. The kicker was seeing past myself, my own fears, and seeing my son living a healthy and happy life as his authentic self.

> AS PARENTS, WE MUST LEARN TO CELEBRATE OUR LGBTQ+ CHILDREN OR WE WILL SUFFER WITH THEM, OR WORSE, WITHOUT THEM.

How did fear and ignorance cloud your perspective on your son's coming out?

I grew up believing homosexuality is a sin and that my son would burn in hell for being gay. Those thoughts are devastating. I felt like I had to choose between my faith and my son. I was frozen in my fears. Add to that, for example when Parker was of age to go to our local gay 39th Street strip, I would beg him not to go alone as I *"knew"* there was an orgy or hate crime waiting to happen in the street. That was my perception of the community and dangers of his "coming out."

How would you encourage other parents not to feel limited by their beliefs when it comes to loving their LGBTQ children unconditionally?

As parents, we must learn to celebrate our LGBTQ+ children or we will suffer with them, or worse, without them. The world is full of faith-based resources on the subject. We know now with the history of human sexuality, evidence, and testimonies from our LGBTQ+

Christians the ONLY choice is to not remain in fear and ignorance of what it means to be gay.

How does your faith inform your love for the LGBTQ community today?

This journey took me from the church to the pride parade without losing my faith and through meeting this beautiful Spirit-filled community I experience God and humanity to a greater degree than I ever thought possible. I can go to a drag show and cry hot tears at the beautiful expression of human sexuality, whereas before I would have thought it perverted or offensive.

Why is the practice of gay conversion therapy dangerous to LGBTQ youth especially?

Conversion therapy (I call it shame-based "ministry") is still legal, sought out, and paid for in Oklahoma. Any form of preaching, teaching, or practice that attempts to change the sexual orientation or identity of another human at any age has PROVEN to be harmful even to the point of death. The practice is criminal and it's time for the good and educated people to say "enough is enough."

How do you hope the message of Free Mom Hugs will seek to educate people about high suicide rates for LGBTQ youth and work to involve more parents in their kids' lives?

Studies show that by having even one supportive individual in the life of a LGBTQ+ person, it can lower the suicide rate by 30 percent. The message of Free Mom Hugs is to encourage the LGBTQ+ community and their parents to live and have authentic relationships, and the more we can do that the more loving, kinder, and safer our world will be for everyone. My hope is that someday we won't need Free Mom Hugs.

Your organization also helps LGBTQ people in practical ways. Can you tell us what you do?

We provide food and gas cards, safe places, and basic needs to those homeless or living at risk because they've been kicked out of their homes for being gay. We help with processing fees for name changes on legal documents for our Transgender friends. We host a Transgender Valentines Banquet, a time to honor our Transgender community and those that love and support them. We provide resources and speak at schools, hospitals, and churches.

We travel with the Free Mom Hugs banner across the country, and are currently preparing for our third Free Mom Hugs Tour of Hope. This is a two-week, ten-city-stop, ten-thousand-hug Tour of Hope, leaving Oklahoma City traveling by Jeep to San Francisco, spending Mother's Day on Castro Street. This trip is inspired by the life of Harvey Milk, calling on people to stand up and speak out in favor of our LGBTQ+ family and friends. I'm doing what I wish someone would have done when I was trying to figure things out. There is a mom like me "back then" who needs a mom like me now.

Do you invite dads as well as other family members to partake in your events?

All are welcome. The only requirement is that participants be affirming.

How do you help other churches and organizations become more supportive of the LGBTQ community?

By educating, sharing our stories, being vocal and visible about celebrating our LGBTQ+ community as an important part of our history and future. The ripple effect of doing these things, I believe, has the power to change the social norm.

Finally, what makes you a powerful woman?

Hope in humanity. Seeking it out like my hair is on fire.

MIA IVES-RUBLEE

JANUARY 21, 2017, SAW PEOPLE MOBILIZE ACROSS THE United States, and around the world, in record-breaking numbers for the inaugural Women's March. What started as an idea among activists angry about the election of Donald Trump turned into one of the biggest modern women's movements we have seen, evidence of the growing momentum around feminism.

One activist in particular decided to lead the way to make sure the disabled community was represented. Mia Ives-Rublee founded the Women's March Disability Caucus. She helped coordinate accessibility services for over forty-one thousand disabled people and ensured that the Women's March was fully inclusive. For her work on the Women's March, Mia was named by *Glamour* magazine as one of 2017's Women of the Year.

Mia is a disabled transracial adoptee who has dedicated her life's work to civil rights activism. She began her journey as an adaptive athlete, competing internationally in track, road racing, fencing, and CrossFit. She obtained her master's in social work and began working with disabled people to help them find work and independence in their communities. She has lectured across the country on issues related to social justice and enabling everyone to participate fully in all aspects of society.

Tell us about growing up in Greensboro, North Carolina, as a transracial adoptee, and how that impacted your identity from a young age.

Growing up in North Carolina felt very isolating. There were no other Asian Americans in my neighborhood and very few in my schools. The ones that were Asian American were primarily in ESL (English as a second language) classes. I had no one who looked like me that I could look up to or get guidance from. I didn't make any real efforts to looking into my Korean identity until college, where I met a really cool person in acting class. She was the first one who helped me reclaim my identity through humor.

How did a trip to the 1996 Paralympics change your outlook on being disabled?

I came to this identity through sports, and my athletic career was really kicked off by the 1996 Paralympic Games in Atlanta. I remember being shocked when we arrived in Atlanta to see all these disabled adults who were just there to celebrate and compete in the games. It was the first time I got to see disability in a positive light. So often, as a disabled person who may have complicated medical issues, you get told you can't do things. Athletics allowed me to push those boundaries that all the adults had set for me. The lighting of the Paralympic torch that year lit a fire in me that has yet to go out. It allows me to push against the limitations people set and look for ways to continue to seek new goals.

When did you start to become more immersed in activism and politics?

College was an amazing experience for me because I got to immerse myself in so many activities. Part of that

THE LIGHTING OF THE PARALYMPIC TORCH THAT YEAR LIT A FIRE IN ME THAT HAS YET TO GO OUT. IT ALLOWS ME TO PUSH AGAINST THE LIMITATIONS PEOPLE SET AND LOOK FOR WAYS TO CONTINUE TO SEEK NEW GOALS.

included socially active theater. We would perform skits for audiences and then talk about the social issues they addressed. I was involved in student leadership, helping remove a racist mascot, and talked about accessibility issues on campus. I also participated in my first march, which was on labor rights for migrant workers.

After obtaining my master's in social work, I began working in my community to help disabled individuals obtain employment. I didn't truly put together how policies affect people's everyday lives until I worked with clients who came back for services because the policies that were in place made them *more* vulnerable. After six years, I decided I could no longer sit in an office and watch the revolving door of clients. That was when I tried out research. I learned quickly that it was not what I was interested in. The research we were doing took too much time and I often wondered how much of it was used to actually improve people's lives.

I was still trying to figure out what I wanted to do when Trump was elected.

Why did you decide to form the Women's March Disability Caucus?

After Trump was elected, I saw some posts online about a Women's March happening in Washington, DC. I had just made a promise to myself that I would get more politically and socially active in my community. Originally, I had only planned to get involved on the state level. I contacted some people that were helping organize a contingent to go from North Carolina to Washington, DC, but didn't hear from anyone.

As I waited, I began noticing Facebook messages on the national March page asking if the event would be accessible. I totally understood why people were concerned, based on my own experiences at marches. When I noticed the messages weren't being replied to, I came up with an idea: What if I organized a group of disabled individuals who were interested in attending and was able to show Women's March organizers that they needed to include disabled people in the policies and event planning? That was how the Women's March Disability Caucus was born.

Mia Ives-Rublee speaks onstage

For those who aren't aware of what the ADA [Americans with Disabilities Act] does, can you explain how has it helped disabled people participate more fully in public spheres?

I am part of the ADA generation who grew up largely after the ADA was signed (in 1990). For disabled people everywhere, the ADA provided legislation that made it illegal to discriminate against disabled people in public accommodations, employment, state and local government services, and telecommunications. It recognized that disabled people should be granted the same rights as nondisabled people.

As part of the ADA generation, it had been instilled in me from a very young age that I deserve the same chances as my peers. This allowed me to focus on my education and gave a framework for my parents to advocate for my rights when school policies and administrative decisions infringed upon them. There was no question that I would try to seek employment after I graduated because of the ADA. While the ADA is not perfect, it did provide a framework that has allowed millions of disabled people to participate more fully in their communities.

Many of the things that are required by the ADA are now seen as conveniences, which has helped make the world more accessible. Everything from curb cuts to elevators to telecommuting. All of these were designed to help disabled people and now nondisabled people can benefit from them also.

You recently wrote a powerful op-ed about the need to include more disability voices in the fight for Medicare for All. Can you tell us what is lacking in this conversation?

For the longest time, health care was a topic ascribed to the disability community because we are the most prolific users of its services. However, we were always seen as customers and never experts. This has led to a continuation of policies that don't truly address our needs. After the health care fight in the summer of 2017, nondisabled people realized that the public was hungry for universal health care coverage. While Medicare for All had been bandied about, few ever thought it would ever make any progress until recently. Now senators and representatives are feeling the pressure to write up more substantiated bills.

In 2017, most of the new health care bills ignored covering services that could greatly benefit disabled people, including Long-term Services and Supports (LTSS). In 2018, through the work of numerous disability advocates and activists, Democratic Congresswoman from Connecticut Rosa DeLauro became the first to create a bill that would cover community LTSS. Democratic Representative from Washington State Pramila Jayapal followed suit, creating a single-payer bill that would include community LTSS. As the largest users of health care, we should have a say on how the health care system is rebuilt so that it covers all people.

Finally, what makes you a powerful woman?

A woman can be powerful in so many ways. I truly admire women who are knocked down, yet continuously get back up again to fight for what they believe in. I admire a woman who is willing to help other women get ahead and I admire women who make sure they get the credit they deserve. I have worked towards these goals all my life and I hope that it reflects in my work.

CASSANDRA BANKSON

CASSANDRA BANKSON IS THE FIRST OF TWO POPULAR YouTubers I chose to include in this book. In a world that is changing so fast when it comes to digital and social media, online influencers have become celebrities in a whole new ecosystem that can seem overwhelming and confusing for some. Cassandra Bankson has over eight hundred thousand subscribers on her self-titled channel, where her videos rack up thousands of views every time she publishes them. Primarily centered around makeup and beauty tutorials, Cassandra's personal brand and channel is so much more than a major makeup company's influencer dream. She has successfully utilized her platform to be a place of encouragement, where she openly discusses her own health issues and relationships and isn't afraid to talk about social impact issues that she is passionate about (animal activism, bullying, LGBTQ issues). Having partnered with large brands such as Ulta Beauty, Amazon, Sephora, and more, Cassandra believes the key to connecting with her global audience is being authentic.

How did you begin your journey into vlogging?

It happened completely by accident. When I was growing up with acne, it was hard for me to make friends. I chose to isolate myself, due to fear and anxiety. Having acne was an insecurity that impacted my life in many physical and emotional ways. As I started to get curious, I watched YouTube videos. Seeing other girls talk so openly on camera about their lives, and teach makeup tricks and eyeshadow looks to girls like me who didn't understand them, really gave me a sense of community. I watched YouTube for four years before creating my own channel. For me, it wasn't about being a blogger. It was about being involved in a community that had given me so much. I never would've expected that my personal perspective of makeup and acne would impact so many people. At the time, acne was not discussed openly. It wasn't until years later I found out that many other people suffer with it but were just as ashamed, and were hiding it the same way I was.

WE ARE FOLLOWED FOR BEING REAL AND RELATABLE, AND ESPECIALLY WHEN WE OPEN UP TO DISCUSS ISSUES THAT WE ALL STRUGGLE WITH, IT HELPS TO NORMALIZE THE CONVERSATION.

You started to get major attention from major mainstream media outlets like Good Morning America after you posted a video talking about your severe acne. What was that like for you?

Good Morning America didn't reach out until two years after I had been blogging. At this time, YouTube was not mainstream—it was still a small website that not many people knew about. For me, it had been my video diary for the past two years. I never would have expected so many people to find my channel, and as wonderful as it was to meet more people interested in speaking about makeup and acne, it was also terrifying. My biggest secret, which had previously been between myself, my camera, and a small YouTube audience, was now being spoken about internationally. That was a lot for me to process emotionally.

You were bullied because of your acne, and today you have become a beacon of hope for so many youth online, especially girls. How does that make you feel?

Acne almost ruined my life. Bullying solidified my own insecurities and gave me negative words to play back in my own head every day.

As horrible and as painful as these things were, my YouTube audience really helped me process so many of these things. Having a community to speak openly to, and discuss things with, was a form of therapy I never could have gotten from a doctor's office. Looking back, I am grateful that I had acne. If this experience didn't shape me, I never would have found my passion for skin care and education. I never would have found my purpose to help others feel beautiful and express themselves confidently to change the world in a better way.

How do you think YouTube and makeup vloggers have been instrumental in spreading messages of self-love and empowerment among youth?

I believe the influencers have led the way when it comes to how advertising and brands react to the marketplace. When I was growing up, I would pick out magazines from the store shelves. Media was not shaped by the general population, it was a set amount of editors and brands who got to choose the images that we saw and determine what was "beautiful" or "ugly." There weren't many checks and balances. With social media, the game has changed because influencers are a different type of celebrity. We are followed for being real and relatable, and especially when we open up to discuss issues that we all struggle with, it helps to normalize the conversation. Every single "like" on social media is a vote. This has become a valuable means of self-expression and changing the way women express and consume beauty. Brands have noticed this and started to create products and advertisements that more accurately reflect what we, as customers and consumers, actually need. I am grateful to be a part of this movement and hope that it shows an example to anyone watching that Beauty is not defined by any standards other than your own.

How do you deal with people who choose to attack and leave nasty comments on your videos?

In the past, this would bother me tremendously, and there was a point where I couldn't read my comments. What I really had to do was find ways to respect myself and love myself for who I am. When I started to recognize who I am, and feel proud of that woman, the things that people said didn't impact me as much. Nowadays, when I get haters I don't even delete their comments. I usually reply with something kind, which makes them even more angry, which in turn makes me giggle! Additionally, I think it can lead to progressive conversations if they are approached from a place of love.

In 2015 you revealed some more major health news—you have uterus didelphys. Can you explain what this is and why it got so much attention in the media?

I was shocked to find out that I had uterus didelphys [a uterine malformation where there is a double uterus with two separate cervixes, and possibly a double vagina as well], as well as only one kidney. Just the way I've spoken about other strange bodily conditions, I decided to share this online. Because it got picked up by some media and TV shows, it went viral. It was only after the fact that I realized that this probably wasn't the best. I wanted to explore the science and the potential connection with acne but the media wanted to talk about how this would make great porn. I'm still glad that I opened up about it, as I realized that there are thousands of other women with the same condition. So many started reaching out to me. I was able to share some information that helped a researcher in the Philippines with a few of his patients that are suffering from UD. Being able to share my experiences honestly with my audience is a freedom that I know was a privilege but I try not to take for granted.

In 2018 you came out to your audience in a video, sharing that you are a lesbian. What has been the response since you released this?

Coming out was one of the most difficult things that I have chosen to do. Similar to my acne, my sexuality was something that I hid for years. Once I had cleared my acne, I thought that my life would be transformed—that I would be confident, feel successful, and feel free. But the truth is that hiding my attraction to women was holding me down. It was frustrating when my friends' parents would ask me why I haven't been looking for someone to date or marry, and they wouldn't understand when I explained that "it's difficult for me." Going out to brunch with a group of girlfriends, including my actual girlfriend, and having to pretend like we weren't in a relationship was very emotionally exhausting for me. I finally recognized that my sexuality wasn't something that I could change or continue to deny. I had shared my life so openly online, and I felt that after coming out to friends and family who did end up accepting me, doing so publicly was the last step.

Finally, what makes you a powerful woman?

I personally believe that knowledge is power—understanding my mistakes, why they happened, and how I can turn them into opportunities for growth allows me to be a better human. I believe my power comes from an unquenchable sense of curiosity, wanting to understand how things work. Asking the difficult questions. Speaking to new people. I also believe that sharing the knowledge that I have online has helped empower others. When we see someone else being unapologetically themselves, it gives us permission to step into our own authentic selves.

ANNA AKANA

ANNA AKANA IS THE EXECUTIVE PRODUCER AND STAR of YouTube Red's original web series *Youth & Consequences*.

Anna's content is the very expression of using the Internet as a tool for female empowerment and activism, as she posts on topics including social justice, reproductive rights, racism, relationships, and more. Anna is Japanese American, and it was extremely important to her to portray a multifaceted, complex, nonstereotypical Asian lead in *Youth & Consequences*, as well as work with a cast that reflects the real world. In the series Anna plays powerful teen trendsetter Farrah Cutney, the queen of Central Rochester High. The show tackles hot-button issues such as the trans/LGBT experience, suicide, bullying, and more, within the confines of the seemingly life-or-death stakes of high school.

I had the opportunity to chat with series star and EP Anna about her role as Farrah, making meaningful YouTube content, and the impact she is passionate about making through her work.

Tell me about the idea behind *Youth & Consequences* and some of the issues it tackles.

I found the script a few years ago and fell in love with it. I've read a lot of high school pilots and films, but none of them tackled adolescence with as much sophistication and elegance as [creator/writer] Jason Ubaldi did. The characters are smart, multidimensional, and constantly keeping you

guessing with their complexity. Jason and I discussed utilizing the microcosm of high school to mirror the social and political issues going on in our society today. We touch on transgender rights (specifically the controversial bathroom laws that had such a huge spotlight on them in 2017), suicide, and privacy and its relationship to social media, as well as gender inequality, power dynamics, and family dysfunction.

You have become well known among the YouTube community as an influencer using her platform to speak about important topics. Why is this important to you?

I believe that the most important thing I have is my voice and what I stand for, as not only an artist but a person. I recall being a young adult and being so influenced by the actors and writers I looked up to. I trusted their opinions and their advice without question. I once read that when a person sees a celebrity, the area in the brain that lights up is the same area that's activated when you see a friend. Without any real interaction at all, artists have the power to touch people emotionally. I take that responsibility seriously. I try to use my platform to be vocal about issues that have personally affected me and that I'm passionate about.

Can you tell us about your focus on suicide prevention?

I'm vocal online about losing my younger sister in 2007 to suicide. Suicide is the third-leading cause of death in teens. *Third.* That statistic always blows my mind. But having dealt with serious clinical depression

> I BELIEVE THAT THE MOST IMPORTANT THING I HAVE IS MY VOICE AND WHAT I STAND FOR, AS NOT ONLY AN ARTIST BUT A PERSON.

myself, I can understand how someone much younger and with less of a reference for time can feel the need to end it all. Jason and I often talk about how high school stakes feel life-or-death because it's the first society you're ever a part of.

When you're only sixteen years old, years seem like eons to you. It's all new and frightening and impossible to know that life is constantly changing, that emotions do eventually pass, and that the people whose opinions you value today may not even be in your life a decade from now. I hope that I can help people through that dark phase in their life and wait it out.

You have close to two million subscribers and over ten million views across your channel. How do you deal with negativity and trolls?

Honestly, at this point I don't even care about them anymore. I've heard the worst insult you can imagine over a hundred times. Plus, I take solace knowing that *no one* would ever speak to me that way face-to-face. I try to empathize that the person on the other end of a mean comment is still a person, and that their reaction has more to do with their own life than what they actually think of me.

As a Japanese American playing the lead in the series, why was it important to reflect real-world demographics in a way that wasn't "tokenistic"?

Though it was a conscious choice, it definitely doesn't *feel* that way on screen. And there's nothing I hate more than a show that feels like it tried too hard to pick one of every color. Everyone on the team agreed that we wanted this show to reflect the world around us because representation matters *so damn much*. Studies have shown that it influences your hobbies, career, even marital status! What you see on screen has real-world implications.

One of my favorite aspects of the show is that the only other Asian American woman is Piper Curda, who plays the puppet I build up who eventually takes me down. Though we're both Asian and the protagonist/antagonist, it never felt like "oh no, two Asians. This is a show about Asians," or that it was women pitted against each other.

You are the star as well as the executive producer of _Youth & Consequences_. What do you think will be the wider impact of seeing more female creators across all platforms in entertainment?

I hope the impact will be to empower women. All the characters in this show are powerful. It's a female ensemble of various types of complex people, and I hope there's one that everyone can relate to. I hope we can showcase women being powerful, vulnerable, sensitive, strong, feminine, masculine, and so much more than just a love interest or the accessory to a man, that it will leave every girl watching with a feeling that they can do the same. After I watched _Wonder Woman_, I left the theater feeling like I could take on a thousand men with my bare hands. It was amazing. I want our show to inspire someone else to make their next project and do the same.

How can the Internet become a tool for female empowerment and intersectionality, more so than even traditional media?

The lack of barriers on the Internet really gives any type of creator a platform. There are so many walls up in traditional media. That's why some of the biggest YouTube stars in its early origins were Asian: Ryan Higa, Natalie Tran, Michelle Phan, HappySlip, Wong Fu. Asians who didn't see themselves on a TV or movie screen could finally identify with people on their computer. We have LGBTQ+ creators amassing huge followings. We have females, particularly women of color like Lilly Singh and Liza Koshy, becoming huge stars. The Internet is a platform that anyone can access, and I think the stars it is generating speaks volumes to what we are lacking in traditional media.

DANNIELLE OWENS-REID

SOME OF THE BEST AND MOST EFFECTIVE SOCIAL changes are made by people who see a gap or an unmet need and resolve to fill it, rather than waiting for someone else to take up the mantle. One of these people is Dan Owens-Reid (who also goes by Dannielle)—an author, speaker, and CEO of a gender-fluid clothing marketplace and inclusion consulting agency called Radimo, where she also represents and manages social media influencers and creators. Dan experienced viral fame earlier in her career via the blog she started in 2010, called *Lesbians Who Look Like Justin Bieber*, which led to the opportunity for her to run social media for Virgin Mobile on tour with Lady Gaga and cofounding the LGBTQ youth organization and highly successful YouTube channel "Everyone is Gay." EIG tackled LGBTQ subjects and enabled parents and youth to utilize the content as a helpful tool for conversation and destigmatization.

Dan's career mission has always been the same—to give visibility to the LGBTQ community in a way that is educational, diverse, and inclusive. Dan's passion to see social change in entertainment and fashion comes at a time when it is more important than ever.

How did you create your management company and why did you launch this?

I kind of fell into it. I was writing for my first client, YouTuber Stevie Boebi. She needed additional help with negotiations/timing/

organization. She had all the brand smarts and I've been in social media and business for nearly a decade. We made a perfect match. She is the one who taught me that no one should have to work without at least some of their payment up front. After about a year of working with her, another influencer friend approached me about management. My goal with both of them was to protect them and get them what they deserve as creators. My focus has always been on those in marginalized communities. I saw how a brand would blatantly offer my white client more money than one of my black clients with the same-size following. Because I managed them both, that was literally unacceptable and I could lay out for the brand exactly what they were doing wrong. In so many cases with my clients, because they're women, queer, trans, black, disabled, plus size, etc., people will try to mess with them, and me stepping in with my white man-sounding name changes the conversation.

IN SO MANY CASES WITH MY CLIENTS, BECAUSE THEY'RE WOMEN, QUEER, TRANS, BLACK, DISABLED, PLUS SIZE, ETC., PEOPLE WILL TRY TO MESS WITH THEM, AND ME STEPPING IN WITH MY WHITE MAN-SOUNDING NAME CHANGES THE CONVERSATION.

Why is it important to you personally to see more queer, trans, black, people of color, women, and disabled creators represented in public spaces?

When I enter a room, event, or workspace and everyone I lay eyes on is cis, white, hetero, able-bodied, I feel really uncomfortable. I grew up poor and most of the white families in my town were very affluent. The white kids thought I was weird and made fun of me, the black kids thought I was funny and were always super nice to me. I think this stuck with me and kind of wired my brain to believe that if there are plenty of people around who all look different, then the room is safe and I'll find a friend.

That wasn't something I consciously understood at the time, or even well into my adulthood. I've worked in many different fields that were meant to be "safe spaces" and at the end of the day still prioritized white creators over everyone else. So many businesses/brands/organizations have access to the funds and creative ideas to make their spaces safe and inclusive. The decision not to do so is an active one, and there's no justified reason for it. People don't realize that by expanding who you represent, you're expanding your customer base.

Radimo is also home to a gender-fluid clothing brand dedicated to challenging the traditional standards of fashion. What kind of items of clothing does it include?

Shirts, shoes, dresses, skirts, shorts, makeup, wellness products, earrings, pendants. We also host brands and products from queer, trans, people of color, nonbinary, disabled, plus size, and women-owned businesses and designers. Every item in the store is photographed on at least three different body types, skin tones, and gender expressions, giving so many of us the opportunity to see ourselves reflected in fashion and the ability to support brands and designers from our own communities.

How can fashion play a powerful role in the self-esteem of someone, especially someone who feels like they don't belong?

Having the ability to wear whatever you want, present however you want, be seen however you want, it's life-changing. I discovered so much about my relationship with my own gender through clothing. I've always hated dresses, I've always hated suits. I've always wanted something in the middle, but never had the words (or clothing) to figure out what that meant. For so long I hated my body because I thought that's what made me feminine. But once I started to dress differently—wearing clothes from both the men's and the women's section—once I started to carry myself differently, changed my hair, changed the people I hung out with, etc., I started being seen as genderqueer and began to love my body in a whole new way.

We hardly see many disabled models in the mainstream. Why is this the case?

I think there are as many disabled models in the mainstream as there are black plus-size trans models. Virtually none. Because when designers are putting clothes on the runway, they want it to look exactly as the clothes would look on a hanger. Having someone extremely thin and extremely pale who can walk quickly and in a straight line is what they care about.

People don't hire disabled models because in their mind, that is a limited experience. They believe there aren't many disabled people in the world (false), and they believe not many of them care about fashion (false). If you want to know what disabled people of color think about fashion, ask them. Brands will be blown away by reality if they just ask.

You used to run the "Everyone is Gay" YouTube channel with your cocreator, and you are the coauthor of *This Is a Book for Parents of Gay Kids*. Was this educational aspect of your work something you always envisioned doing?

My dad says ever since I was a kid, I've always cared about what's fair. I absolutely love giving advice and I love motivating people to know that you can just love each other.

I created the *Lesbians Who Look Like Justin Bieber* blog for laughs and almost immediately people were asking me really deep questions. I used to call it "accidental activism" because I never thought of myself as an activist simply for telling a parent that it's cool to still love your gay kid. People were so confused because their church or pastor or whoever told them, "no you can't love your gay kid," but these parents truly felt like they still did. They were lost and it didn't feel like education for me to just say, "ok, so what if you just love your kid anyway?"—it just felt right.

Gender identity is a very big topic and can often be used to divide people politically with terms like "identity politics." How do you change this dynamic through your work?

I never believe that someone should have to defend their identity. "Identity politics" is just someone's way of saying, "I don't want to respect you so I won't." I think if we focus our energy on the friends, family, businesses that are making the effort, we will see ourselves thrive on a personal and global level.

The consulting that I do with brands, corporations, and influencers focuses on just that. I facilitate workshops, but I am not the only consultant. I bring in five to seven additional consultants from all different backgrounds—race, body type, disability, gender—their life experiences are different from mine and together we build programs with the brand to make their business, products, online, and overall brand messaging completely inclusive.

Finally, what makes you a powerful woman?

Being a powerful woman to me was about dropping every single expectation I was taught about who I needed to be. I feel like I grew up understanding I just had to be less powerful.

As soon as I knew my gender was up to me and my career was up to me and my partner was up to me, that's when I felt powerful. I saw what society gave me and said, "No thanks! I'll be doing this my own way."

HABEN GIRMA

HABEN GIRMA IS A TRUE WONDER WOMAN AND A trailblazer in her own right. In 2013 Haben became the first deafblind student to graduate from Harvard Law School, and today as a civil rights attorney and activist she has helped the forward momentum in the fight for greater and more robust disability rights. Born and raised in Oakland, California before first setting off for college in Portland, Haben has family roots in Eritrea, a country from which her mother escaped into Sudan as a refugee to flee political strife. Haben's mother was determined to give her daughter a life of success in America where she could have the chance to thrive.

During her school and college years Haben realized the importance of special education materials for disabled students that can be the difference between an equal education and one that potentially holds them back. Haben learned to speak up for herself and learned how to harness the power of advocacy for change. Although she never had any grand plans to be an activist of sorts, eventually her path would lead her to this calling.

As a lawyer, Haben most notably won a very important case representing the National Federation for the Blind against digital library company Scribd, a case that outlines why disability inclusion and advocacy impacts so many areas of society, including technology, media, and education.

Today Haben is an in-demand advocate, being asked to speak at various events and conferences and with different organizations around the world.

Haben Girma (right) with Stephanie Syptak-Ramnath

You are the first deafblind student to graduate from Harvard Law School, which makes you a pioneer. Do you feel a responsibility to ensure there are more educational opportunities for students with disabilities?

I want to use my skills and talents to increase opportunities for students with disabilities. Advocacy is a choice. I'm choosing to serve as an advocate. People with disabilities should have the choice whether to use their time to advocate for disability access, gender equality, protecting our planet, and other missions.

You are a civil rights attorney advocating for disability rights and raising awareness about the need for better accessibility. Was law and advocacy something you had always dreamed of pursuing?

Not at all. I didn't know what I wanted to major in when I started college. The decision to go to law school occurred near the end of my time at college.

Growing up in Oakland, you have spoken about how supportive teachers and classmates, as well as materials that helped you learn, made a big impact on your path to college. Would you say every child with disabilities has the same type of accessibility in school in the United States?

The access I experienced went above and beyond what most students with disabilities experience. I wish more schools provided access for students with disabilities. Improving education access requires schools to invest in access. The local and federal government needs to provide schools with more funding to support access, and schools need to use the funding to increase opportunities for students. The culture needs to change, too. Teachers and school administrators need to treat disabled students as students worth teaching.

As a lawyer a case you won on behalf of the National Federation of the Blind brought up larger conversations about the need for more technology companies to innovate in a more inclusive way. Can you tell us more about this?

I represented the National Federation of the Blind in a lawsuit seeking to get the digital library Scribd to make its services accessible. Because of the design of the Scribd website and apps, blind readers could not access many of the books and documents. Scribd argued that it didn't have to make its services accessible, claiming the ADA [Americans with Disabilities Act—a civil rights law that prohibits discrimination against people with disabilities] doesn't apply to websites and apps. Disagreeing with Scribd, the court ruled in our favor. "Now that the Internet plays such a critical role in the personal and professional lives of Americans, excluding disabled persons from access to covered entities that use it as their principal means of reaching the public would defeat the purpose of this important civil rights legislation," the court wrote. Scribd soon agreed to make its digital library accessible. Working on this groundbreaking case to help blind readers gain access to books was one of the most rewarding moments in my legal career.

Tech companies need to make accessibility a priority. In 2016 I stopped litigating cases to focus instead on educating organizations on the benefits of choosing to practice inclusion.

[Information included in this answer regarding the court case also came from Haben Girma's website and is used with permission.]

Among your advocacy work is your passion to ensure media representation of disabled people is more inclusive and less

clichéd. How does the media play a larger role in how people view the disabled community and how they are treated?

When films and shows have "disabled" characters, they are usually nondisabled actors pretending to be disabled. Casting directors should recognize talented disabled actors. We are not one-dimensional beings. We are multidimensional, part of many communities, and living with numerous talents and interests. Stories should reflect that.

How do you think social media and the blogosphere has enabled more people within the disabled community to share their stories and concerns with a wider audience?

Accessible social media platforms amplify voices we rarely hear. There are still aspects of social media that are not accessible, though. For example, a lot of podcasts and videos don't have transcripts.

Many photos online do not include image descriptions. Add image descriptions when posting images online so that blind individuals can access the content of the photos. If people want to add a hidden image description they can now do that, but most people still don't write image descriptions.

MY ADVOCACY WILL LEAD ME THROUGH UNEXPECTED ADVENTURES, AND I LOOK FORWARD TO THE JOURNEY.

What are some good disability rights organizations that people can follow and support?

The Disability Visibility Project is a good one.

Where do you see yourself in ten years?

In ten years I see myself pleasantly surprised. I have no desire to follow a traditional career path. My advocacy will lead me through unexpected adventures, and I look forward to the journey.

Finally, what makes you a powerful woman?

Many people try to hide their challenges. My power comes from owning my challenges and working to find alternative solutions.

WOMEN OF
THE ARTS

THROUGHOUT MY LIFE I HAVE ALWAYS BEEN DRAWN TO entertainment and art—whether it be the grunge music that defined my angsty teen years in Australian suburbia, or the iconic films and movie stars that set me on a pathway in television and media that eventually led me to Hollywood in 2008, it has been the backdrop, the driving force, and even the healing balm for my life.

As a young girl, growing up in Australia in my Indian family and being part of a religious community, art seemed to transcend any awkward identity I couldn't quite wrap my mind around. It was my mother's passion for powerful stories in Indian arthouse films about real-life struggles Indian women faced, which would set the early stage for my own passion as a fierce advocate for women's voices and stories.

Art and entertainment changes the world. Pakistani-Canadian filmmaker Sharmeen Obaid-Chinoy is a great example. She is a two-time Academy Award winner. Her 2016 film *A Girl in the River: The Price of Forgiveness* won Best Documentary, Short Subject at the eighty-eighth Academy Awards and followed the story of a nineteen-year-old girl who survives an honor killing attempt by her father and uncle, simply for falling in love with a boy. After watching a screening, Pakistani Prime Minister Nawaz Sharif pledged to put a stop to this, and asked his team to redraft laws on honor killings to help ensure that perpetrators are punished and victims are protected.

The creative industry is a vital tool for women across the world today because it has been a way to highlight injustice, but inequality also exists within industries themselves.

Out of the top one hundred grossing films of 2018, women represented only 4 percent of directors, and Kathryn Bigelow is still the only woman to ever win the Academy Award for Best Director.

In a study about the voices of men versus women in news media in the United States, the Women's Media Center found that at twenty of the nation's top news outlets, men produced 62.3 percent of news reports while women produced 37.7 percent of news reports, which gives you an idea of how news media shapes narratives about what is happening in culture today. According to ProductionPro, out of 233 principal roles on Broadway, only 37 percent were female, and only 19 percent of directors in these productions were women.

It's clear we have a long way to go to find equal representation. How do we get to a place where we see more women and female-identifying voices in the mainstream art and entertainment world having an impact on culture and society in a way that men have enjoyed for a long time? Awareness of the numbers and problem is the beginning; working to make change is key.

In this chapter you will meet incredible, badass, and inspiring women who are paving a new path for emerging voices, most notably their own.

SARAH MOSHMAN

I'VE KNOWN EMMY AWARD-WINNING FILMMAKER SARAH Moshman for six years and I cannot say enough great things about her. Sarah hails from Evanston, Illinois, and has seen her work screened around the world, filmed around the world, but she is having a powerful impact on individuals in such a personal way.

Her most notable films include *Losing Sight of Shore*, following the journey of four women who rowed unassisted across the Pacific Ocean from California to Australia (available on Netflix worldwide); *The Empowerment Project*, showcasing pioneer women who are disrupting the status quo in a number of industries; and her latest project, *Nevertheless*, tackling sexual harassment in the workplace. Sarah is also a mom, a film teacher, and a speaker.

Sarah's ambitions and successes are a reminder that with persistence, authenticity, and an ambition that is undeterred by the circumstances, anything is possible.

What is your earliest memory of wanting to be a filmmaker and make a career out of directing?

The first documentary I made was in high school for an English class; it was about unique family dynamics in my community. I enjoyed the process of taking an idea and using the camera to ask questions of others I might not have the courage to ask otherwise, and then sharing the completed film with an audience. I think from then on I knew I wanted to be a filmmaker in some capacity as a career.

Taking that initial leap out into the unknown can be scary for so many people, especially women. How did you get the courage to do that with your career?

I was working in reality television for my first five years living in Los Angeles, mainly as a field producer for ABC's *Dancing with the Stars*. It was a great job, but I wanted more out of my career and I was feeling the itch to create my own work. The quote that helped me around that time was: "Sometimes you climb the ladder of success to find it was on the wrong wall."

It's easy to get caught up in what other people define as success. For me, being able to create my own opportunities and shine a light on stories that have meaning to me and to the world was something I was hungry for and I decided to take a leap of faith and start making documentaries. I had no idea if it would work out, but I had to at least see what I was capable of!

IT'S EASY TO GET CAUGHT UP IN WHAT OTHER PEOPLE DEFINE AS SUCCESS.

What made you decide to focus on creating films centered around women's stories?

I started to really become aware of the way we treat women in the media around 2012 after working professionally in television for a handful of years. It was clear that women are oversexualized, objectified, ignored, and not allowed to be fully complex, real, and flawed characters in our stories. Women are not often the heroes; they are the sidekick, the girlfriend, etc. I was hungry for more content where women get to be front and center.

I wanted to create more media that I wished I had seen when I was younger. That's really how my first feature film, *The Empowerment Project: Ordinary Women Doing Extraordinary Things,* came about—I and four other female filmmakers got in a minivan and drove across the

United States to interview inspirational women in all different career fields.

Tell me about the process of making *Losing Sight of Shore* and why it is about SO much more than just rowing.

Losing Sight of Shore was truly one of the great adventures of my life. I was introduced to the rowers, the Coxless Crew, less than three months before they were to set off across the Pacific Ocean, so I had barely any time to get ready for this journey. I bought the rowers cameras, hard drives, and microphones so they could tell their own story at sea and then I would meet them along the way on land at certain points and film them coming in from another boat with a drone or helicopter above!

The journey took nine months in total. I knew people would want to watch this story unfold. I struggled so much to raise the money to finish the film, I invested a lot of my own money, brought on investors, I was awarded four grants (after countless rejections), and more. It was a true test for me as well, and even though I didn't physically row the ocean, I too crossed a "Pacific."

The story was always so much more than rowing to me; it was about the power of the human spirit and what we are all capable of when we push ourselves to the limit.

What are some things you have learned about sexual harassment from the characters in *Nevertheless*?

I'd say it's clearer to me more than ever that this is such a systemic issue. We can't look at one bad apple, or one company and expect them to fix the problem. We need to be thinking bigger in the sense that sexual harassment exists in a pyramid whose foundation is built upon objectification and offensive remarks, and at the top is rape and assault. We can't "solve" sexual harassment without addressing the entire pyramid. The film examines the ways in which our legal system can fail victims, the way we socialize our girls and boys differently, as well as the way the brain reacts to trauma and taking a look at the long-term effects of these behaviors.

In its simplest form, this is about respect and kindness. If we can encourage the people around us to stop making offensive remarks that dehumanize women, especially in the workplace—then little by little we do change the culture. And vowing to not be bystanders. If we see someone else being harassed then we have the power to step in as well. I'm also learning so much about great men in this space that are true allies and advocates and are encouraging other men in their circles to do the same. I believe we can do a lot of good with shifting culture and sparking important dialogues in workplaces around the world with this film.

If there was one thing you could tell every up-and-coming female filmmaker today, what would it be?

I would say don't wait for this moment where you think you're going to feel 100 percent ready or qualified to make a film. You are the only person you need to get permission from to get started. You are capable of more than you know! So what are you waiting for?!

What makes you a powerful woman?

I'm a powerful woman because first of all, I birthed a human. Mothers are powerful.

I'm also a powerful woman because I create my own opportunities and I don't wait for others to pick me. And I want to help as many women as I can along the way.

VIOLETA AYALA

FILMMAKERS, ARTISTS, AND STORYTELLERS
HAVE ALWAYS BEEN POWERFUL VEHICLES
FOR TRUTH. DOCUMENTARIES ESPECIALLY
HAVE THE POTENTIAL TO SHIFT CULTURE
AND CHALLENGE PERSPECTIVES IN A WAY
POLITICS PERHAPS CANNOT.
BOLIVIAN FILMMAKER VIOLETA AYALA AND
HER AWARD-WINNING FILMS ARE PROOF
OF THIS. HER DOCUMENTARIES *COCAINE
PRISON* AND *THE FIGHT* HAVE EXPOSED
AUDIENCES TO ISSUES IN A WHOLE NEW
WAY THAT MIGHT NOT HAVE BEEN POSSIBLE
THROUGH TRADITIONAL NEWS MEDIA
OUTLETS. HER PRODUCTION COMPANY,
UNITED NOTION FILMS, WAS FOUNDED IN
2005 WITH HER FILMMAKING PARTNER
DAN FALLSHAW WITH THE INTENT TO
"CHALLENGE THE STATUS QUO."

COCAINE PRISON, RELEASED IN 2017, OFFERS A VIEW into the lives of everyday people in prison for transporting cocaine. While shows like Netflix's *Narcos* showcase Pablo Escobar and various drug cartels, in Bolivia, the culture around the coca leaves is very different. It is a plant that has virtually no taboo surrounding it (it is as normal as growing coffee beans and is a very common plant that farmers harvest), and it is legal to grow up to a certain amount.

However, transporting it is not, and people risk being thrown into prison by doing so. But in communities where there is poverty, cocaine transportation is a job that brings in money even for teenagers. The Bolivian government enforces drug laws, which allows it to charge powerless drug workers while often turning a blind eye to powerful "big fish." As a result, half of all prison inmates in Bolivia are in for minor drug offenses.

In her film Violeta puts a human face on the vicious circle of life in and outside the notorious San Sebastian Prison. *Cocaine Prison* follows Daisy, a teenager who struggles to escape the lure to traffic cocaine; her brother Hernan, arrested with two kilos of cocaine near the Argentinian border; and his best friend Mario, a cocaine worker fighting for freedom. Not a stereotypical prison, San Sebastian is more of an overcrowded, government-run slum holding seven hundred people, most of them in legal limbo. Violeta and Dan managed to smuggle in cameras to various inmates. *Cocaine Prison* is a rare case of a prison documentary partially shot by the inmates themselves.

"The universal truth of the War on Drugs is that it targets the most vulnerable everywhere: the drug workers at one end and the drug addicts on the other. They are the ones who are called criminals. But the world economy runs on drug money. And the key players, the big fish, live outside justice. The justice system is based on money, class, and race," said Violeta.

She spent four years making the film, which had a personal aspect to it because of her own Indigenous background.

"We, the indigenous people from the Andes, have lived with the coca leaf for millennia. It was a white man who, in 1859, made cocaine and now it is the powerful people in the West who profit the most while we risk our lives," she said.

Violeta explained how she was sick of seeing the stereotypical portrayal of cocaine traffickers and also wanted to show the stories of those in prison from an Indigenous lens.

"There is a difference between white people filming other cultures, as they don't often view them as equal," she said.

Showing these prisoners as humans, not just tropes or characters, was deliberate, and while the reception from young people has been mostly positive, Violeta says it has confused critics, who are most likely used to seeing the *Narcos* version of the cocaine trafficking trade on screen, because it doesn't fit their predeter-

mined narrative. *Cocaine Prison* is showing a side to the drug trafficking industry that doesn't get enough attention, and Violeta is the one making sure more people see this.

But it's not just the drug issue Violeta has tackled. After making *Cocaine Prison*, she came across a group of disabled activists who were protesting the Bolivian government and President Evo Morales. After becoming intrigued by their mission to stop discrimination against the disabled community through policies, Violeta picked up her camera once again and decided to document their work. This ended up becoming the acclaimed short film *The Fight*, which was distributed by *The Guardian*.

People with disabilities are among the most discriminated against in Bolivia. Fed up with being ignored, a group of them marched across the Andes to the government in La Paz, asking to speak to President Evo Morales. They were met with riot police, barricades, tear gas, and water cannons. Violent confrontations flared up between police and the protesters, with officers using pepper spray and water cannons. The government refused to discuss their request for a pension of seventy dollars a month and the protesters suspended themselves from the city's bridges in their wheelchairs. After following the protesters on the march, Violeta and Dan gained intimate access to their camp, including up-close scenes of regular violent reactions from the police. The filmmakers and other journalists were also threatened. For three months the disabled activists attempted to speak to the president but faced criticism from the state's official news outlets.

Violeta says that President Morales, once seen as heralding the dawn of a new political leadership as the first Indigenous president, has slowly gained control over many aspects of politics as well as the media, and it has become almost impossible to get a true sense of the issues disabled people are facing from local media, which has essentially become a state-run medium. Violeta used the power of social media to write about what she was seeing and filming for The Huffington Post to spread more awareness about what the media refused to show. And of course she used her filmmaking skills as a weapon against political oppression.

I HOPE THE NEW GENERATION SEES US AS PEOPLE, NOT STRANGE CREATURES.

"Bolivia used to be a lot freer in terms of expression, but that is being taken away by the government," said Violeta.

Violeta comes from a family of activists—her grandfather was a political prisoner for his views—and now she is using film to take on the establishment.

The disabled activists have been raising awareness about children being abandoned by their parents for their disability and those living in poverty because of their physical condition. The activists Violeta followed are asking for better government benefits, yet political leaders have accused them of devising a strategy to "destabilize the government," according to *The Guardian*.

Violeta says the reason President Morales and his government are afraid of giving these activists what they want and allowing them to have any power is because they think it will embolden other activist groups to rise up and potentially push back against government control. If the disabled people are empowered to protest for what they want, able-bodied people could do even more, is the thinking.

Since *The Fight* was released, there have been some major changes for the activists in Bolivia. President Morales introduced a bill in Congress allowing a small monthly monetary benefit to people with severe disabilities. It was only half the amount the activists were asking for, and activists weren't overjoyed with the gesture. One of the leaders of the group, Rose Mery Guarita, said the more important achievement was to raise awareness and respect.

"With the protests, we have managed to make the general population more sensitive. I hope the new generation sees us as people, not strange creatures," she said.

The protests have gained worldwide attention thanks to Violeta's film. She also traveled to Geneva and stood before the United Nations assembly denouncing Bolivia's treatment of the disabled people. Yet she gives all the praise to the group of activists who have worked tirelessly for their community.

"These protesters are smart, they are political, and they know exactly what they are doing," said the filmmaker.

The Fight has helped change the narrative about the disabled population as well as the government in Bolivia in a drastic manner. Violeta says the ability to shape public discourse, especially as an Indigenous woman, is why storytelling is important to her.

"The media is the most powerful tool in terms of controlling people, by telling the same narratives. But we have to change that. We need more women of color and Indigenous people telling their own stories in their own ways," she said.

INDIRA CESARINE

MANY PEOPLE THINK ART AND ENTERTAINMENT ARE "liberal" industries, allowing for creative people to define the rules and break them as they see fit. But when you look behind the curtain you start to see a very different picture being painted in terms of how power is structured. Visibility and representation are not as democratic as you'd think, and this is especially true in the art world.

Today, only 30 percent of artists represented in commercial galleries in the United States are women, and that figure decreases in countries like China, Hong Kong, and Germany. Only 13 percent of living artists represented in galleries in Europe and North America are women.

Yet the stats show that women make up 51 percent of visual artists in the United States.

If the problem here is accessibility and opportunity, then surely one of the easiest solutions would be more female-owned galleries and women heading up gallery and museum budgets.

One particular artist and gallery owner herself is determined to change the status quo in the art world and has been using her space to showcase artists that share messages about intersectional feminism, gender equality, and challenging the norms.

Indira Cesarine is a multimedia artist who has worked in photography, video, painting, printmaking, and sculpture. After spending fifteen years in the US and abroad as a photographer, she

shifted her focus from fashion to contemporary art. Initially she launched a digital magazine that would showcase video and print artwork, and in 2014 she opened her own gallery in New York City called The Untitled Space. Indira is an artist with a vision, a mission, and a focus on making art a space that is truly inclusive, not afraid of being political when it needs to be.

You first worked in fashion and photography before jumping over to contemporary art. What made you switch gears?

I ended up pursuing photography after college because I felt more confident that I could have a "career" as a fashion photographer. The art world at that time was very difficult to access if you didn't have connections. I did my first shoot for British *Vogue* when I was only twenty-five, and over the years I shot a lot of covers for top magazines, as well as advertising for the likes of Kenzo, Charles Jourdan, and Dior.

After working as a photographer for fifteen years, I started to feel like I wasn't pushing myself anymore. The industry had shifted from film to digital, and it became far more commercial. I wanted my work to have more meaning. The industry was also very male-dominated. It wasn't easy to get work.

In 2008, during the financial crisis, I decided to move back to New York. I ended up launching an indie magazine just for fun. We were producing and creating everything and I had a lot of interest from other photographers, directors, and artists to collaborate. It inspired me to go back to my love of painting and printmaking and continue to explore my work as a feminist artist. In 2015, I curated my first all-female exhibit, "The F Word: Feminism In Art," which featured twenty artists. It was such a positive experience, I was inspired to create a platform to continue the exhibitions. I transitioned my former photo studio into The Untitled Space gallery and here we are today.

I THINK IT'S IMPORTANT TO LOOK AT HISTORICAL NARRATIVES THAT WE MAY TAKE FOR GRANTED, BUT ARE EQUALLY EMBEDDED IN OUR CULTURE AND HAVE HAD LASTING IMPACT.

As a female artist and gallery owner what are some of the barriers you have had to navigate so far in your career?

I always struggled to get work as a photographer in the American market. It was almost impossible as a woman to get a good agent or commissions. Most agents only represented one female photographer compared to ten or twenty men. When I transitioned to art, I found that it was equally challenging for female artists to get representation—most of the galleries in New York represented 90 percent male artists. I started curating my own exhibits of all-female artists, because there weren't that many opportunities for women unless you created them yourself.

When I first started curating exhibits for The Untitled Space, a lot of the female artists did not want to align with "feminism" or even be labeled a "female artist." That has changed over the last few years, between the Women's March, as well as with the #MeToo and #TimesUp campaigns.

I think a huge turning point for The Untitled Space gallery was presenting the "UPRISE/ANGRY WOMEN" exhibit, which featured eighty female artists responding to the political climate in America and

Trump's election. I knew after that exhibit, despite how hard it can be running an art gallery, that I had to keep going—not only with my own work as a feminist artist, but also supporting other female artists and having a platform for feminist art.

Many of the exhibitions at The Untitled Space explore sex and sexuality through the female gaze. Why is this important to you?

Part of the equality equation is eradicating the double standard that women can't enjoy and celebrate their sexuality. Despite the women's sexual liberation movement of the 1960s and 1970s, the double standards still exist. It has always been an important part of my work to challenge gender stereotypes. We have so many deeply rooted sexist narratives that promote a male-dominated society, it is important to look beneath the surface and investigate what our culture considers "normal," such as Trump's "locker room talk," or words such as "slut" or "bitch" that put women down. As a feminist artist, I think it's important to celebrate sex-positive femininity.

Why are you passionate about challenging the status quo?

I think it's important to look at historical narratives that we may take for granted, but are equally embedded in our culture and have had lasting impact. In 2019 I presented an exhibition, titled "EDEN," that investigated the story of the Garden of Eden. Aside from the gender stereotypes, role of subservience, guilt, and blame it has placed on women, the story of Adam and Eve has positioned women as "inferior" to men since the beginning of time. I felt it was time to take a look at this story from a feminist perspective.

How can more female and female-identifying artists support one another in order to gain access to more financial opportunities?

In the past few years there has been a lot of all-female exhibitions and female artists are getting more exposure, but that needs to be translated into sales. I have seen an increase in collectors acquiring the work of female artists in the past few years, but you can see from public auction records that male artists still dominate the art market. Only two works by women have ever broken into the top one hundred auction sales for paintings.

There are a lot of ways artists can engage and support one another, whether it's launching your own fiscally sponsored project, putting together a collective, or just encouraging more collectors to buy art made by women.

Culturally, women have been raised to be competitive with one another, and that needs to change. We need to rally together to teach our friends and follow artists that being supportive is far more effective for progress, and to break these financial barriers, rather than being competitive.

Finally, what makes you a powerful woman?

I don't always feel powerful. Sometimes I feel vulnerable and frustrated. I try to channel my feelings into my artwork and my exhibitions. A large part of my work is confronting social norms that have held women back. It takes a lot of confidence and energy to rally behind issues that can often be controversial. People are not always supportive. At the end of the day, you have to trust your instincts, and follow the path that you know to be true. I think that is where we can all find our inner power.

CATHERINE SCHREIBER

IF YOU ARE EVER IN DOUBT ABOUT THE POWER OF ART and entertainment to change hearts and minds, then you need to get familiar with Broadway producer Catherine Schreiber. She is a trailblazer who didn't follow any of the conventional "rules" that the theater world demands.

She didn't start her career on Broadway, but ended up pivoting at a stage in her life when the entertainment world seems to write off women (a good reference for this is Amy Schumer's "Last F***able Day" comedy sketch). Today, the two-time Tony Award–winning producer, who has over twenty-five major productions both in the United States and abroad under her belt, doesn't show any signs of slowing down.

Through some of her most notable productions, including the award-winning *The Scottsboro Boys,* which tackles history, race, and the Civil Rights movement, Catherine spoke to me about how she is most passionate about working on plays and musicals that have the ability to move the cultural needle on topics such as race and sexuality.

She is the first woman to win the prestigious Broadway Global Producer of the Year award, showing that the world should never write off women and what we are capable of achieving with the right amount of passion and motivation. But beyond all the accolades and industry recognition is a woman who cares deeply about the work she is doing and how theater can play a major role in helping to change the world for the better.

How did you pivot your career into Broadway after the age of fifty?

I grew up in New York, and lived in the city pursuing an acting career. After that I went to Los Angeles to find work. I met my husband, started a family, all while pursuing acting and writing. I wrote solo and with a writing partner. Several films were optioned and developed.

We worked with Sony, Disney, and Kate Hudson's company, among others. We had so much fun with one script, "Desperate Writers," that we decided to make it into a play. I hadn't been on-stage in twenty years before "Desperate Writers." When we moved to New York, my hope was to produce "Desperate Writers" there. I was introduced to a manager and producer who said if I wanted to get involved in producing a show in New York, I should invest in a Broadway show for a learning experience. He was producing *Next Fall* at the time. I said, "I don't want to invest, I want to produce." Here was a show about an important subject: homosexuality and the resistance of institutions like hospitals to acknowledge a homosexual relationship when it came to visitation rights, etc. This ticked off a key box for me in terms of important issues. So I went for it. That was my first Broadway producing experience. *Next Fall* was nominated for four Tony Awards, including Best New Play in 2010. That was how my Broadway producing career began.

Within eight years you garnered two Tony wins, six Tony nominations, five Olivier Award nominations, and have to date produced over twenty-five plays and musicals. Which production did you get most excited about?

The show which I've been most excited about is Kander and Ebb's *The Scottsboro Boys*. This musical, directed by Tony and Olivier Award winner Susan Stroman, is about the nine teenage black youth, ages thirteen to eighteen, who were wrongly accused of rape in 1931 segregated Alabama. Their trials led to two seminal Supreme Court rulings that decided that everyone deserves proper representation and is entitled to be judged by a jury of one's peers. In that case, black people could not be prevented from serving on a jury. It actually helped spark the Civil Rights movement in the United States. Rosa Parks met her husband at a Scottsboro Boys rally.

In 2013, I was honored again when I delivered the keynote speech at the signing of the Scottsboro Boys Act to exonerate the boys. [Former Alabama] Governor Robert Bentley said I had helped to change history.

Now that is what theater is about! It can change attitudes and lead to more understanding, empathy, and compassion. Theater provides an opportunity for everyone of all races and economic groups to see their lives, their struggles, depicted onstage.

The show changed my life.

THEATER PROVIDES AN OPPORTUNITY FOR EVERYONE OF ALL RACES AND ECONOMIC GROUPS TO SEE THEIR LIVES, THEIR STRUGGLES, DEPICTED ONSTAGE.

Can you tell us about some of the women who inspire you on Broadway?

One of the first women I worked with was Nelle Nugent, a wonderful producer, mentor, woman. I loved her inclusivity and her desire to get all coproducers to share their expertise in trying to make a show succeed. Stacey Mindich brought *Dear Evan Hansen* to Broadway. Jill Furman (*Hamilton*), Daryl Roth (*Kinky Boots*), Robyn Goodman (*Avenue Q*), Barbara Whitman (*Fun Home*), Ruth Hendel (*Fela*), and more. And of course there is London-based Sonia Friedman, whose scope of work and success is now legendary. I am thrilled to be working with her on *Dreamgirls* in London. All these women are all terrific producers.

What would you say to especially the woman out there who is feeling lost in her career, doesn't know which direction to turn because of her age, but wants to do something meaningful?

One: Forget age. Two: What are you passionate about? What gives you joy? What makes you happy? If you love the theater, get involved with the theaters in your area, support them, get on their committees. If you love Broadway, seek out the shows you love, see who produced them and reach out to them. Maybe invest or try to produce. Don't let anyone say you can't do anything. I plan on working in theater until I can't work anymore. Age means nothing.

MAYTAL GILBOA
AND THE WOMEN OF EMET COMICS

WHEN YOU THINK OF COMIC BOOKS, YOU THINK OF DC or Marvel, and characters like Batman, Superman, Ironman, and the rest. It has traditionally been a testosterone-fueled landscape in terms of creators, writers, editors, and illustrators, as well as the fans. But with 50 percent of comic book readers today being female, there is a massive market of a previously untapped audience.

We've all seen the way Marvel and DC are honing in on the female empowerment movement on the big and small screens—with the *Wonder Woman* movie, for example. In comic books themselves, the popularity of the new "Ms. Marvel," who is now a Muslim Pakistani American teen girl, and the female Thor storyline speak directly to the changing market. But there are also independent, female-run, minority-driven companies making change from the ground up.

One of these is a comic book company based out of Los Angeles whose focus is female characters, writers, and illustrators, all day, every day. Emet Comics was founded by a former film industry executive, Maytal Gilboa, who left her job to create a platform that celebrates female artists, and also infiltrates the nonfiction comic book world with incredible diverse stories that are often hard to come by. When I first found out about Emet Comics I knew immediately that this was a company I need to get familiar with.

Maytal Gilboa
FOUNDER, EMET COMICS

What is Emet Comics and how was it created?

Emet Comics is a packager and financier of comic books and graphic novels focused on empowering female creators from different media backgrounds. My personal background is in film and television development and I recognized the lack of opportunities for women in these fields. My hope was that we could create a unique space for women to tell their stories without the obstacles we often face in the mainstream media.

What makes it different from other comic book companies?

Most of us come from film backgrounds and we aren't considered traditional comic book fans. We read indie comics and graphic novels but we don't necessarily rush to the comic book store every week to buy the latest releases. We have a longer development process. We explore new ideas and styles. We are not afraid to take risks and experiment with the medium.

There is still a perception that women don't read comics, or aren't interested in them. What are some facts to counter that myth?

While comic book store sales are only growing by 4 to 5 percent each year, there has been a huge increase in digital downloads and a 16 percent increase in book markets. Diversity, women, and kids are driving these trends. Barnes and Noble doubled their graphic novel section over the past few years.

Series like *Jessica Jones* and *Supergirl* are giving female comic book characters a mainstream platform like never before. How do you hope this will help more women gravitate toward comics?

Powerful role models change how we think about ourselves and our abilities. I consider the creators of these shows just as influential to the empowerment movement as the characters themselves. Women need to be able to see themselves as creators/directors/showrunners in the same way that women and girls need to see themselves as Supergirl. My hope is that as more women break out in these fields, more women will want to work in them, and as a result there will be more interesting content and more role models behind and in front of the scenes.

Melissa Jane Osborne *AUTHOR*, THE WENDY PROJECT

Tell us about your journey to becoming a comic book writer.

I'm an actor and a playwright/screenwriter by trade, so it's been a very unexpected journey. I never thought I'd write a comic. I met with Maytal, pitched her an idea, and she suggested it would make a good comic. So suddenly I was writing a comic book! Coming from a theater background my way in was to treat the book like an artifact (her diary). It's been a new way for me to think about storytelling and I have respect for comic writers after this experience.

POWERFUL ROLE MODELS CHANGE HOW WE THINK ABOUT OURSELVES AND OUR ABILITIES.

The Wendy Project is a twist on a popular children's story. Can you tell me why you chose to focus on Wendy's POV?

The original J.M. Barrie story is called *Peter and Wendy*, not *Peter Pan*, but somehow along the line she got pushed to a side character, and an extension of him. Really, if you look at the story Peter couldn't exist without a Wendy to believe in him. I wanted to reframe that and ask how she could believe in herself. She was always the most interesting part of the story to me. She was a complex girl who was caught in between these two worlds, who was relegated to mothering this selfish man-boy. It struck me that a modern teen girl now would be a little more discerning and freaked out by this guy in tights.

What are some of the barriers you have faced as a female writer?

My first agent out of college told me not to speak after auditions, because my "intellect didn't match my aesthetic" … I'm a blonde girl who loves wearing dresses, and I think people have a stereotype of a female writer that I don't match. I've been in auditions with actors reading my work who didn't realize I wrote the material. As a woman it's challenging to own and be empowered by my feminine qualities. I also think people pigeonhole you into female-driven content. I want to create stories with inspiring, complex, messy people of all genders.

What advice would you give girls who want to become writers?

One day it's going to suck, and then you're going to think you're a genius, and the next day it's going to suck again, but if you keep doing it something has to happen. Make sure you only share that early work with people you really trust. There's nothing that can crush a great idea better than sharing it with the wrong person before it has a chance to grow.

Cindy Tobisman AUTHOR, INSIDE THE LOOP

Tell me about the futuristic setting and story of *Inside the Loop.*

Inside the Loop tells the story of two strange cities and a damaged hero that must save both. The outer ring, the Collective, is a regimented world run by an all-powerful Administrator. The inner ring, the Loop, is a thug-capitalist tenement divided among seven Bosses. These cities have nothing in common except for the Plague, a disease that regularly decimates each city's population.

Tora Welborne is a survivor of the Plague. Once a badass detective in the Collective, she returns from Quarantine to investigate whether the Loop's crime bosses are using the Plague virus to destabilize the Collective. But survivors of the Plague are pariahs and Tora's homecoming is rough. When she's forced to sneak into the Loop to find the technology necessary to cure herself, Tora must kick butt, solve the mystery of the Plague, and stop a war.

What made you want to be a comic book writer?

The comic book world is brave and experimental and bold in a way other media is not. Seeing a story rendered in images is powerful. I love the collaborative process of writing a story and watching the talented Lynne Yoshi turn my words into something beautiful and visual. Images and words, coming together to create mood and tell a story, is unbelievably cool.

Also, I'm a novelist, so I'm used to having tons of space to tell a story. Writing a comic book forces me to focus on what matters. Learning to tell the essential story is a really useful discipline for anyone who likes telling stories.

What do you think is missing in pop culture when it comes to female characters?

Pop culture is improving, but it's still got a long way to go in depicting female characters that are as nuanced and complex as male characters. Women are often portrayed through the lens of how men see them. I think that's often true. The best way to change the depiction of female characters is to get out there and create the content you want to see.

Jean Barker *AUTHOR, ZANA*

Your comic book tells a reimagining of the apartheid story but with a difference. What did you change from the original setting?

It's set in a future in which apartheid wasn't defeated by a revolution because Nelson Mandela was executed instead of imprisoned. Instead, it's taken over all of Africa and it's now 2084.

How did growing up in South Africa during the apartheid years shape your view on gender, race, and identity as you grew up and moved to the United States?

My parents hid apartheid from me as a young child. But you could feel it in the air, and by the time I was ten, I knew. I think it taught me a lack of faith in any authority, or any system. I'll never accept the idea that it's right "just because it's the law," or "because it's traditional," having grown up to see that it's often very wrong.

There is a dearth of diverse characters in comic books and even mainstream entertainment. How do you hope to change that through your writing?

South Africa is diverse, and so is Zana, and the two characters at the center are black, or one is mixed, depending how you define that. In the context of the story, Zana being biracial is definitely important. It was less a deliberate choice than it was the story that sprang to mind. I want to represent the world as I see it, a world in which "white" is not the default. That's not what I see around me anywhere in the world. But turn on the TV and it's tokenism at best, although that's finally beginning to change.

LAVERNE DELGADO

ONE OF THE MOST UNIVERSAL VALUES THAT EVERY human being on the planet wants to experience is freedom. Freedom looks different to each individual, but for some it can be the difference between life and death, success or slavery. An organization based out of Los Angeles called Freedom & Fashion has been working to help majority female victims of sex trafficking since 2008. They help survivors using fashion and beauty to empower youth in overcoming trafficking, homelessness, and other injustices. They operate three programs and hold an annual fashion show where the survivors get to show off their newly fostered creative talents to an audience.

Freedom & Fashion is deeply conscious that helping survivors of the sex trade means more than just helping them escape a bad situation. They need help to rebuild their lives and set up a support system that allows them to be emotionally, financially, and physically stable. With the help of multiple partner organizations they are able to offer job-training skills in combination with imperative conversations addressing self-image, vulnerability, leadership, character development, and more. Program director Laverne Delgado understands what it means to be a survivor firsthand, as she has escaped multiple situations of abuse throughout her life. Her passion for the work F&F is doing comes from a place of personal acknowledgment that there is always a way to use your pain for a good purpose. Her purpose is to help other survivors find freedom through creative avenues, restoring their dignity and purpose in life.

How did you initially get involved with Freedom & Fashion?

I came on as a Program Director to create our direct impact programs. Up to that point, Freedom & Fashion was an awareness platform, so I was excited to help our organization get to a new level of service.

Although Americans talk a lot about "freedom," the truth is that many people in this nation are currently living in captivity. What are some stats that people should be aware of?

- ✧ Human trafficking is the second most lucrative organized crime in the world. America is not only a global destination, we have a rampant sex culture and we are leaders in consumerism.
- ✧ As many as twenty thousand kids are forced into prostitution by human trafficking networks every year.
- ✧ One in three young people are solicited for sex within forty-eight hours of running away or being homeless in the United States.
- ✧ The average age of a teen entering the sex trade is twelve to fourteen years old.
- ✧ California is home to three of the FBI's thirteen highest child sex trafficking areas in the nation: Los Angeles, San Francisco, and San Diego.

How do former victims become part of the F&F organization?

There are many stages in the rescue/rehabilitation process. We partner with other organizations that rescue survivors and house them. Partnerships are a massive part of our impact. We provide our program to homes, shelters, schools, etc. that are rehabilitating survivors.

Part of rebuilding the identity and life of a survivor is enabling them to be financially stable and find a new purpose. How does F&F address this?

Our programming goes beyond fashion and the expression of art. We explore trade-driven industries while engaging in imperative

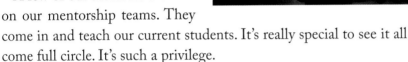

conversations addressing self-image, vulnerability, leadership, character development, and more. By combining creative job training with coaching methodology, our programs strengthen the right hemisphere of the brain, which enables our students to create a new vision and accomplish aggressive goals.

A few of our survivors are now on our mentorship teams. They come in and teach our current students. It's really special to see it all come full circle. It's such a privilege.

Tell me about the annual fashion shows and how the survivors take part in this.

Our Freedom & Fashion Annual Fashion Show is a celebration of our youth's power, creativity, and uniqueness. By showcasing our students' designs, we praise their journeys and completion of our programs.

From creative direction to design to ambiance, this show is 100 percent inspired by our students and their stories. Open to the public, this unique and powerful experience gives the community an opportunity to show their support by investing in the programs that follow.

IT'S REALLY SPECIAL TO SEE IT ALL COME FULL CIRCLE. IT'S SUCH A PRIVILEGE.

What are some of the backgrounds and situations that these survivors have escaped from?

Since the start of our direct impacts programs, we've served nearly five hundred youth and women. Some of the most sobering stories are those of young girls. I had a thirteen-year-old girl who was trafficked by her grandmother since the age of six, and this was in Los Angeles.

Another girl we served was seventeen and she escaped one of the most dangerous cartels in Mexico. She was taken when she was a child, enslaved, and forced to have sex with multiple men a day for years. When she refused, they stabbed her and shaved her skin with a machete. She and a friend tried to escape and managed to get away, but not without being shot. Her friend didn't make it. Lucy watched her get gunned down and die in front of her.

The girls and women we serve are literally warriors. They are the strongest people on earth.

Would you be willing to share any of your personal story that motivated you to want to help others?

I have my own story of abuse and I knew early on I was going to use those experiences to help others. My survival has been dependent on giving purpose to my pain. I've gone through a lot of trauma, from sexual abuse as a child to an abusive marriage. There have been many moments when I wanted to give up on it all, but the courage of our students kept me going. If they can face their pain, and push through, so can I. They inspire me every day.

Why did you decide to stay with F&F for as long as you have?

Freedom & Fashion is growing and it's fun to be part of the impact with my team! I also created our programs so there's a sense of ownership there. When I see our students transform, I feel a sense of joy, unlike anything I've felt before. I know there is a lot of pain out there but I also know healing is available to us all if we choose it. Seeing our students choose healing day after day fuels my passion and keeps me going.

Finally, what makes you a powerful woman?

My commitment to truth and health. I pursue the integrity of every situation, which has led to a lot of pain, growth, and healing. The truth isn't always pretty, but I face it head on to move forward.

WOMEN WHO
DEFY THE ODDS

I LOVE THE QUOTE "WELL-BEHAVED WOMEN SELDOM make history," which often gets attributed in pop culture to Eleanor Roosevelt or Marilyn Monroe. For me, growing up being told I was rebellious or stubborn, it was like finding the reason for why I was so determined to be different and question the norms around me. It made me realize that it wasn't about being a "troublemaker," but was an indication that I had a desire to change things for the better.

When I think of women who defy the odds, I don't think it's possible to fit them into one particular box. The women I've chosen to include in this chapter have beaten social stigma as teen mothers to have a successful career, defied oppressive political regimes to create media designed to amplify women's voices, and overcome a life-changing medical diagnosis.

What unites all of these stories is the way these interviewees have embarked on their various journeys for the sake of also helping numerous other women around them. They have tread new pathways, creating opportunities for many other people. They have bared their wounds, proudly owned their scars, and fiercely and determinedly walk through life not being afraid of the challenges ahead.

RAOFA AHRARY

THIS IS A STORY ABOUT A PIONEER WOMAN
AND A TESTAMENT TO THE VALUE OF
MEDIA, ESPECIALLY IN COUNTRIES WHERE
IT BECOMES THE ONLY VOICE FOR PEOPLE
WHO ARE NOT BEING HEARD BY THE REST OF
THE WORLD.

RAOFA AHRARY HAILS FROM AFGHANISTAN
AND NOW LIVES IN THE UNITED STATES WITH
MEMBERS OF HER FAMILY, INCLUDING HER
DAUGHTER ARIYA, WHO REACHED OUT TO
ME ON TWITTER TO LET ME KNOW ABOUT
HER MOTHER, WHO WORKED ON ONE OF THE
FIRST WOMEN'S MAGAZINES IN AFGHANISTAN.

*ARIYA TRANSLATED THIS CONVERSATION
ON BEHALF OF HER MOTHER.*

Raofa Ahrary (left) with Ariya Ahrary

AFGHANISTAN IS TECHNICALLY A DEMOCRACY AND NO longer run by the Taliban, but it is still very much a place where women's rights are not automatic, and equal opportunities are still being fought for. Raofa grew up under multiple instances of political strife. In 1975 President Dawood Khan overthrew King Zahir Shah. Then in the late 1970s the Communist regime took over and assassinated President Khan. Raofa's husband Fazal Ahmad Ahrary, a university professor, was taken to a political prison along with other professors in 1979. In 2012 the Dutch government located the war criminals who imprisoned innocent people and killed them in the Pule Charkhi prison in the early 1980s. Among the five thousand prisoners rescued was Raofa's husband, as well as many students and women.

"My life experiences were not easy. I had to escape Afghanistan when my children were teenagers and my daughter was five years old. We needed to sneak out of Afghanistan during the Russian war. My oldest and youngest son went to Germany first with other family members. I and two other sons went to Iran, trying to meet my other sons in Germany later. Iran was at war with Iraq at that time. I then learned my two sons went to the US to make a living instead. My other three children then snuck into Pakistan, living in different houses, and waited until we were accepted as refugees in the US," Raofa said.

Being an educated family, the Ahrarys made the decision to flee to ensure their children would have opportunities that were not as easily accessible in Afghanistan anymore because of the war.

"When politics was about to change to Communism we knew we were in danger. Many opposed it and some were for it. There was a huge political divide. When the Russians invaded it got dangerous. When my husband never came back from prison it was time for me and my four sons and daughters to escape. I did not want my sons to be drafted to war to be forced to fight on either side. We were not a war family. We were about education and college and I did not want my children to die," said Raofa.

Raofa grew up focused on her education, which she knew would be vital in her life as a woman.

"I studied Persian/Dari literature along with Persian philosophy and history of literature. I enjoyed going to school and learning poetry and telling stories to family. Not many women went to school, but they learned on their own," she said.

Raofa was lucky enough to grow up not feeling limited by gender barriers.

"In my family education was very important. There were no colleges in Herat, my home city, so I went to Kabul to go to the University. I was married by then. My husband went to study pharmacy and I decided on literature. It was in our genes to get an education no matter what gender you were. My parents made all of us go to school. There was no double standard," she explained.

Raofa began working at a women's magazine called *Mehrie*. *Mehrie* was an important vehicle for women's issues. It was the first magazine in the Herat area and was sponsored by the government.

"The magazine was about marriages in Afghanistan. Poetry that other women wrote. Sometimes people wrote about women's history in Afghanistan. Many schools were named after educated women around Afghanistan. There were educational topics about women's health, such as pregnancy and puberty," she said.

Raofa says media has always been important to women in Afghanistan, as it has enabled more of them to speak up about what they are facing.

"Women are finding help by watching the media and seeing there are others like them who are brave to come forward about rape or forced marriages. There are more girls on television discussing women's topics. Those who have TV learn a lot. The media in Afghanistan is getting better," she said.

Now that she has lived in the United States for a couple of decades and seen the influence of media in everyday life here, Raofa has learned about the different types of struggles women face. In fact, she has even become aware of certain rights that women had in Afghanistan even before women in the United States!

"I see there are a lot of women's issues we need to deal with in the US. I learned women were not allowed to own property nor vote in the US until 1920. Even though in Afghanistan there was monarchy, the women had many rights to own property and become leaders. Since my family were feminists, meaning men and women were equal, I thought it was the same in the US. Not a lot of families in Afghanistan were like my family, where they treated both their sons and daughters equal. I always thought the US gave women equal rights until I learned recently that women get paid less than men. I would not stand for that," she said.

I TRY TO INFLUENCE MY CHILDREN TO BE KIND AND NEVER SAY NO WHEN IT COMES TO HELPING OTHERS.

Raofa says having a foundation based on education goes a long way to empowering women to raise their voices, even from an early age. Faced with death, war, oppression, jail, and failing health (she is a cancer survivor), she is able to unflinchingly express the importance of women's voices in public life. This pioneer woman is a living example of what happens when women are given the opportunity to change the world. Not just in Afghanistan, but in every country.

"My children wanted to be educated like my husband and me. I try to influence my children to be kind and never say no when it comes to helping others," Raofa told us.

One voice raised gives another voice the courage it needs to also speak up.

JANNICA OLIN

WHAT WOULD YOU DO IF THAT WHICH DEFINES YOU was suddenly taken away? Who would you be? What if your dreams and ambitions hinged on your physical appearance above all else? These are difficult questions that would shake anyone's identity, especially women and girls. It's important to see major celebrities take a stand when it comes to disrupting typical beauty standards (think Alicia Keys and her "No Makeup Movement," for example), but it's also very powerful when we see women in our own communities who we can relate to personally. One woman in particular was confronted with the above questions and ended up learning the power of personal strength and resilience.

Jannica Olin is a Swedish actress, TEDx speaker, and activist based in Los Angeles who has transformed her big screen ambitions into a multifaceted journey where she is inspiring others. In 2014 she learned she had alopecia, which is a condition stemming from a confused immune system that causes all your hair to fall out. As a tall, blonde, attractive Swede setting out to conquer Hollywood, Jannica's sense of identity and self-worth underwent a major reckoning due to alopecia.

Today she uses her platform and extensive social media following to speak messages of power and beauty to others with alopecia, especially young girls. And Jannica has not given up her acting dreams either. In fact, she has discovered a superpower that has opened up numerous doors in a way that perhaps would not have before 2014.

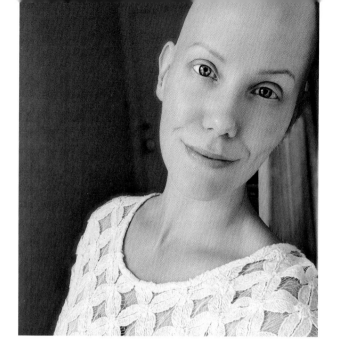

Tell me about growing up in Sweden and moving to Hollywood to become an actress.

I grew up in a smaller town and always felt that desire to discover the world. The dreams of Hollywood started early. I always knew that I would end up in Los Angeles, but I wasn't in any rush to get there. I did some work in Sweden before I took off for Australia. From there I moved to New York after falling in love with the Meisner technique in an acting class.

After New York, I moved to London and worked in theater and film there. After about two years in London, I made my way to Los Angeles.

I had good, professional training in my back pocket and had already worked in theater and film in New York and Europe. There are no quick ways to success. I didn't have solid plans when I got to Los Angeles. I just knew this was where I wanted to be.

How did you deal with alopecia after getting diagnosed?

I discovered a bald patch in August 2013 and six months later, all my hair was gone. The doctors told me it was an autoimmune condition called alopecia, which means my immune system is super strong and super confused and treats my hair as a foreign object. So my immune system is "healing" me from my hair basically. That's the only physical thing that happens. Emotionally, it was a whole different ordeal.

How did alopecia affect your identity?

So much of my identity was in my long, blonde hair and to all of a sudden not have any was very confronting. But I realized something very powerful. It was only when I looked at myself in the mirror that I was different. My thoughts, feelings, and emotions were the same they'd always been. That's when I realized that I wasn't my hair, and if I wasn't my hair, I wasn't my body either. I *have* it. There was a lot of freedom in that. Of course I have thoughts that are disempowering sometimes, but I know that they are only thoughts and not reality.

They're thoughts that are born out of what we take in through social media, culture, and advertising. I started seeing that I had an opportunity to help redefine what our idea of beauty, perfect, and "normal" is supposed to look like. That became my superpower.

ONE REALLY BEAUTIFUL THING IS THAT MY OWN IDEA OF BEAUTY HAS EXPANDED.

What were some of the most profound things you learned about yourself after losing your hair?

I learned that I am resilient. I was losing my hair. That was all that was happening. It wasn't easy to deal with, but I always had a deep faith that this was going to be a blessing. One really beautiful thing is that my own idea of beauty has expanded. I really love short hairstyles on women, which I never used to before.

Because that isn't typically what is considered feminine or "attractive" in our mainstream culture. I've also learned that no one cares about the details of your appearance more than you. For example, I lost all my eyelashes and I've gotten more compliments on my eyes than I ever did before! And I have had to show people that I don't have eyelashes because no one believed me.

How did losing all your hair open up unique opportunities for you as an actress?

There are people in the industry that don't quite know how to cast me. I love going out for roles now that I never would have before, when I had that "girl next door" look. In the beginning when I realized I was going bald, I really thought my career was over. Or that I was going to have to hide with a wig that looked just like my own hair. My job opportunities now have nothing to do with my look, really. Ultimately, it's about who I am *being* about how I look. I love my new normal.

What is your message to people who feel they don't "measure up" to the beauty standards in the world?

To recognize the thoughts and know that you have been conditioned to them by your upbringing, society, media, culture, and history. There's no one single truth when it comes to beauty. Even though we live as if there is. I wish it could be as easy as just "Love yourself." People really are absolutely irresistible and gorgeous when they own who they are.

What makes you a powerful woman?

My resilience and love for vulnerability. Vulnerability is power. And beauty. I always want to be someone who inspires others to step into their power and love who they are.

FARIDA D

FARIDA D IS AN ARAB GENDER RESEARCHER WHO HAS BEEN STUDYING ARAB WOMEN'S EVERYDAY OPPRESSIONS FOR OVER A DECADE. THROUGHOUT THE PROCESS, SHE BROKE UP WITH HER HIJAB AND SET ALL OF HER HIGH HEELS ON FIRE. HER MEMOIR, *RANTS OF A REBEL ARAB FEMINIST*, IS NOW ON SALE ON AMAZON, AND SHE RECENTLY RELEASED A BOOK OF POETRY CALLED *SHIT THAT MADE ME A FEMINIST*. OUT OF SAFETY CONCERNS SHE DOES NOT REVEAL HER FULL NAME OR THE LOCATION SHE IS BASED OUT OF, WHICH MAKES HER FEMINIST WRITING ALL THE MORE BRAVE AND IMPORTANT. WHEN YOU READ HER WORK, NOT ONLY DO YOU GET A UNIQUE GLIMPSE INTO THE LIVES OF ARAB WOMEN, YOU ALSO GET A SENSE OF HOW ALIKE WE ALL ARE DESPITE COMING FROM DIFFERENT PARTS OF THE WORLD.

I HATE SILENCE. YOU WOULD TOO IF YOU WERE FORCED to wear it over your voice and your body every single day. Silence is not just an absence of sound; it is a lifestyle for Arab women. I remember being a teenager, blasting MTV on the highest volume so that I could hear Britney Spears sing at the top of her lungs while dancing around in nothing but her bra, mini skirt, and bright lipstick. Of course now, with the brain of a critical feminist, I view such pop music videos as a reinforcement of female objectification. But back then, to my teenage self, watching a young woman strip off every ounce of her silence was liberating. I come from a part of the world where women are not supposed to laugh out loud in public, because the sound of their laughter may sexually entice men. Women are covered from head to toe, because their mere existence may sexually entice men. Women are seen as sex objects—thus they are repressed and oppressed, hidden under the bondage of silence. Growing up, silence haunted every critical thought in my head and every disobedient inch of my skin that dared to escape from layers of drape. I was reminded of silence whenever I tried to leave it. Whenever I asked seemingly despicable things like: why should I carry the burden of covering my body when it is men who cannot control themselves? Do you know how many "covered women" are still harassed and raped? Why can't I go out late, alone? Make choices about my own life? I could not even post a Facebook status that had slight critical undertones without being warned from well-meaning friends who want me to be publicly silent so that I could still join them abroad at bars instead of being locked behind bars. Yes, Arab women have been sentenced to jail for the crime of posting a defiant status on social media. The silencing police live in our communities, inside our heads, and on the edges of our keyboards. At some point in my early twenties I got sick of speaking to people, and instead began to write. Uncensored. Anything that crossed my mind and I knew would be hushed off if spoken out loud. Being a woman in the Arab world meant there is not one particular patriarchal

> GROWING UP, SILENCE HAUNTED EVERY CRITICAL THOUGHT IN MY HEAD AND EVERY DISOBEDIENT INCH OF MY SKIN THAT DARED TO ESCAPE FROM LAYERS OF DRAPE.

issue to fight against. I wrote about the extraordinary things that happen in the life of ordinary Arab women. My qualification as a gender researcher provided me with the skills and tools to observe and document the everyday opp-ressions we experienced. From issues that women all over the world experience, to subjects spe-cific to Arab cultures; from how we feel about our boobs and bras, dealing with society viewing our

periods as dirty, grooming rules, diet culture, makeup, fashion, the male gaze, modesty, the crime of falling in love, and arranged marriages, to the obsessions with hymens, fear of sex, forced motherhood, shaming of postpartum bodies, sexual harassment, victim blaming, slut shaming, discrimination in the workplace, and more. I criticized the ridiculous religious rulings on issues such as wearing bras and makeup, plucking our eyebrows and pubic hair, having sex, going out without a male guardian, and the sin of praying while wearing nail polish. I wrote about how the sexual objectification of women breeds a culture of terrorists who blow themselves up for the promise of seventy-two virgins in an afterlife, and why I believe Arab men need feminism too. I poured my heart and my rage out on paper.

At first, I kept a journal near my bed where I jotted down my rants and ramblings at the end of each day. I was a Carrie Bradshaw; observing by day, and writing at night. Except, I lived in a city of forced abstinence, and my notes were buried in my nightstand. Also, she wore Manolos so that she can walk seductively. I wore Converse so that I can run away quickly. With time, the need to write became the drug that would get me going through my patriarchy-dominated days. The bedtime journal became a mini notebook I carried everywhere with me, stopping to scribble my frustrations at every opportunity. I constantly took notes during the day and then uploaded them to my laptop when I got home at night. It was liberating to be able to "speak" my thoughts without being interrupted, silenced, or jailed. After seven years of writing, and feeling inspired by my favorite feminist writers, I decided to publish my rants in a memoir and began the gruesome process of editing. I sent out proposals to both Western- and Middle Eastern–based publishers. After a long wait, the rejection letters came pouring in. I expected rejections from Middle Eastern publishers—after all, I was an Arab woman attempting to shatter the silence that surrounds tabooed topics. But I was surprised when some of the Western publishers also rejected my work, providing me with the same rationale as Arab publishers—"although your topic is important, the way you write about it is disrespectful to Arab culture." I found myself struggling to edit myself for others' approval. I could not censor the raw truth and frustrations that many Arab women experience, and have been silenced for way too long. This is not just my voice—it is our voice. I decided that I will not be silenced. Thus, I self-published my memoir on Amazon. Towards the end of August 2018, I gave birth to my book, *Rants of a Rebel Arab Feminist*, and brought my words to life for the world to read. Within a few days, my book began to sell. I have sold copies all around the world, including in the United States, United Kingdom, France, Germany, and Japan. I firmly believe reading and writing are weapons that Arab women may use to arm themselves in fighting the patriarchy. Reading provides me with an escape from an oppressed reality, and allows me to think in unrestricted capacity, all the while hushing the silencing policing in my head. Writing, on the other hand, is a therapeutic process. My pen has become my solace and voice in a land where women are silenced. It is no secret that Arab women who speak out against culture, religion, government, or patriarchy are punished, jailed, or even killed. For now, I cannot stand on the rooftops and scream for a revolution without the risk of being killed. But I can write and pour all my rage on paper, and if they do kill me because of that—I will rest knowing my voice will still live on. Because writers always leave a part of them alive long after they are gone. Writers never die.

BETTY LAMARR

IF YOU DON'T KNOW WHO BETTY LAMARR IS YET, IT'S time to get familiar. Once you learn about her story you will reject every stereotype you know about teen moms, low-income women, and single mothers. Betty is the CEO and founder of a nonprofit based in Los Angeles called EmpowHer Institute, an award-winning organization whose mission is to empower marginalized girls and young women by helping them gain the skills necessary through education, training, and mentorship.

They work to reduce the school dropout rate among marginalized girls from seventh to twelfth grade who are at risk of educational failure due to teen pregnancy, truancy, and juvenile delinquency. Workshops with female mentors engage the girls to know what is possible beyond what they can see in their current circumstances.

Betty created EmpowHer because she once was one of the girls she mentors today. She managed to take her own experience as a teen mom, was determined to finish college, ascended the ladder of success in corporate America, and then decided her highest calling was to give back. The impact she is making on her community in Los Angeles is undeniable.

First, let's talk about your upbringing.

I grew up in the segregated South, in a small southern town in Arkansas called Pine Bluff. At thirteen, I moved to Compton,

California, with my grandparents to get a better opportunity for education and ultimately a career. I had mixed feelings about living in this big city. In spite of it all I was away from my parents and my family, which made me grow up sooner than I should have.

I WAS ABLE TO PUSH THROUGH BECAUSE I WAS DETERMINED TO NOT LET MY CIRCUMSTANCES DEFINE MY DESTINY, AND MY SON WAS MY MOTIVATION.

Your high school graduation experience was different from many others because you were pregnant. What was that like for you?

I was very disappointed in myself because I had dreams of joining a sorority and going to college. Instead, I went to my "shotgun wedding" so that my child would not be born out of wedlock. We had those kinds of morals back then. I became a wife instead of a college student, and soon-to-be mother. It wasn't easy. I wasn't prepared to be a wife or a mother. Instead of choosing a path, it chose me. It wasn't until two years later that I left the marriage and then I began to make decisions that would create a better life for me and my son.

Less than 2 percent of teen moms end up getting a college degree by the age of thirty in the United States. What were some of the difficulties you faced in your education?

I had my college degree by twenty-five and a job offer to join corporate America as an IBM sales representative. Yes, there were some twists and turns along the way. I had to find child care for my son and I also worked at night and went to school during the day. As a single parent, I wanted to make sure he had what I could only imagine. I was able to send him to private school to avoid the gangs and drugs of our neighborhood. After a few years in my corporate job, I was able to move us to the suburbs so he could ride his bicycle on the sidewalk without getting hijacked by the bullies. I was able to push through because I was determined to not let my circumstances define my destiny, and my son was my motivation.

106 *TODAY'S WONDER WOMEN*

At the height of your corporate career, you decided to shift gears and moved to South Africa for a few years. What did you do there?

While in my corporate job, I achieved a great deal of success and blazed a lot of trails as the first African American woman in a number of positions. With this success, I assumed a lot of responsibility for opening doors for other women and minorities. This experience opened my eyes to social issues locally and internationally.

It was this backdrop, along with the joy of seeing my son graduate from an Ivy League university, that inspired me to give back in a bigger way. I was aware of the oppression of indigenous people in South Africa and the opportunity to be a part of rebuilding the country after the first "free elections" opened up to me. I went to share my business knowledge, create jobs, train people, and become a role model.

While doing that, I was inspired by the spirit of the people and how resilient, resourceful, and forgiving they were. I began to see that it is the simple things that bring happiness. I saw how the women created economic viability for their families through their entrepreneurial skills. I saw how they had learned not to expect a job but to create one for themselves. In South Africa, I got more than I gave.

How did this experience spark the idea for the EmpowHer Institute?

It helped me to see how families support each other and how women and girls take the lead in their families for earning money, cooking, and raising the children. This inspired some thoughts about how we can take these lessons of independence and resilience to the teens in major cities in the USA to keep them from dropping out of school. This was the genesis of EmpowHer five years after I returned from South Africa. I could see how pride in what you do raises your self-esteem. It becomes a self-fulfilling prophecy. If you think you can, you will.

What was the need you saw in your community among young women?

I recognized that there are lots of opportunities to help. I saw that black and Latina girls were dropping out of high school at an alarming rate of 50 percent. When I looked at how that contributes to the poverty cycle and a generation of joblessness and homelessness, I knew that I had to do something about it.

Can you explain how poverty can render someone powerless from succeeding?

The thing to remember about poverty is that it can be changed. Most of us are not born impoverished. We have to think about the surroundings and the things people in poverty situations are exposed to. When you wake up every day and you are worried about your basic needs for food, shelter, and safety, that does not give you room to dream about tomorrow because you are trying to make it minute by minute. When girls and women are in vulnerable situations it can quickly turn to hopelessness.

How does mentorship have the power to change people's lives?

I was inspired to go back to school after marriage, baby, and divorce as a teen because I met someone who saw something in me that I didn't see in myself. I listened and figured out how to go back to school based on his encouragement. Mentors are caring individuals who want to help others succeed. They are valuable because they have walked the path you are trying to travel. When I give career advice to adults or teen girls, I suggest that they identify mentors for various stages of their life.

Finally, what makes you a powerful woman?

My authenticity and my comfort with making choices to be all that I am. Showing up as the little girl from Arkansas, the teen mom, and the CEO, all at once. This didn't happen overnight; it took spiritual and professional development to let go of any shame and recognize that all of my experiences made me stronger.

SAHAR PAZ

SAHAR PAZ IS A WOMAN WHO UNDERSTANDS THE POWER OF USING YOUR VOICE FOR CHANGE. SHE WAS BORN IN IRAN AND HAD TO FLEE TO THE UNITED STATES WITH MEMBERS OF HER FAMILY WHEN THE REVOLUTION HAPPENED IN 1979. THE FIRST EIGHT YEARS OF HER LIFE SHE GREW UP AMIDST THE IRAN–IRAQ WAR—AN EXPERIENCE THAT WOULD IMPACT AND SHAPE THE REST OF HER LIFE. AFTER MOVING TO THE STATES, SHE SPENT YEARS BATTLING DEPRESSION, SUICIDE ATTEMPTS, AND TOXIC RELATIONSHIPS, ALL WHILE TRYING TO FORM HER CAREER PATH IN A COUNTRY WHERE SHE STRADDLED A MULTICULTURAL IDENTITY. SHE STARTED OUT IN THE FASHION INDUSTRY AND EVENTUALLY MADE HER WAY FROM COLORADO TO FLORIDA AND THEN TO NEW YORK, WHERE SHE EARNED HER DEGREE IN FASHION MARKETING AT LIM COLLEGE. GRADUATING SUMMA CUM LAUDE

DURING THE FINANCIAL CRISIS OF 2008, SAHAR
WENT ON TO LAUNCH FREE YOUR STAR
FOUNDATION, AN ORGANIZATION WHERE SHE
WROTE AND ADMINISTERED CURRICULA FOR
CREDIT-EARNING FASHION PROGRAMS FOR
NEW YORK HIGH SCHOOLS. SAHAR'S MESSAGE
EVENTUALLY EVOLVED FROM FASHION TO
FINDING YOUR VOICE WHEN SHE WAS OFFERED
A BOOK PUBLISHING CONTRACT. IN 2014 HER
MEMOIR AND REFLECTION GUIDE *FIND YOUR
VOICE: THE LIFE YOU CRAVE IS A CONVERSATION
AWAY* WAS PUBLISHED. THROUGH HER OWN
PERSONAL JOURNEY AND PROFESSIONAL
EXPERIENCES, SAHAR REALIZED HER UNIQUE
POSITION IN BEING ABLE TO HELP OTHERS
LEVERAGE THEIR LEADERSHIP SKILLS TO HAVE
EMOTIONALLY INTELLIGENT CONVERSATIONS
WITH THEIR CLIENTS ALL WHILE MAKING A
SOCIAL IMPACT. IN 2018 SHE LAUNCHED OWN
YOUR VOICE STRATEGY FIRM WITH AN ONLINE
PROFESSIONAL DEVELOPMENT PROGRAM
NAMED VOICE OF IMPACT TO EQUIP TODAY'S
LEADERS TO BUILD AND BRAND THEMSELVES AS
CONSCIOUS LEADERS. TODAY, SAHAR IS BASED
OUT OF HOUSTON WITH A MISSION TO BUILD
A COLLECTIVE OF THOUGHT LEADERS WHO
WILL TIP THE SCALES TOWARDS CONSCIOUS
CAPITALISM.

I WAS SIX OR SEVEN YEARS OLD WHEN I ASKED MY older cousin Parvaneh why everyone was so sad all the time. I don't remember her answer but she recently reminded me how much I surprised her by asking her such a question at a young age. My mom did a good job of sheltering me from my father's attitude and temperament within our home after the Iranian Revolution. When I wasn't in school Mom would shuffle me from our apartment, across the hall to our neighbors and down one floor to my grandparents.

We moved from Tehran to Denver in the summer of 1986 without my father. Mom, brother, and I moved in with my uncle and his American wife in an upper-middle-class neighborhood, where we lived for our first year as refugees of war. Shy of eight years old, I learned just as much from what people said as I did the unsaid. I felt on an emotional, physical, and intuitive level the uncomfortable feelings that my family's presence brought out in folks in public and inside the walls of where we lived. I wondered why we traveled so far to only be imprisoned by another suffocating point of view.

Years before the bombs of the Iran-Iraq war were aimed at Tehran, the Islamic Revolution had already set off land mines within the psyche of its people. Fear through absolutes. Black-and-white was the way of thinking pressed upon my community, along with the introduction and solidification of women as second-class citizens in the minds of both men and women. My first summer in Denver I was introduced to American culture from a very one-sided view that felt oddly familiar. Cloaked in fear, I was told to stop speaking my native tongue (Farsi), and to never mention where I was from—"say Turkey instead." It was made very clear to me that I should act and dress a certain way. Sure, I was able to give up the drab headscarves for pink corduroys, but my place in the world was pretty much the same—second place. Conditioned. Shamed.

The next fifteen years of growing up in Denver I was in an internal tug-of-war, learning and unlearning the conditioning of who I was supposed to be and who I truly wanted to be.

The pattern and prison of pleasing others wasn't something that I had to face until I was twenty-one years old. I found myself, an "empowered" young woman, in an abusive relationship. To my circle of friends, I was the one with a voice, the mature one who had already experienced leadership roles in her career. It didn't make sense to them. And, it didn't make sense to me either.

> I LEARNED AT TWENTY-ONE HOW IMPORTANT IT IS TO HAVE ONE PERSON IN YOUR LIFE THAT IS GROUNDED ENOUGH TO CHAMPION THE MAGIC IN YOU.

I learned at twenty-one how important it is to have one person in your life that is grounded enough to champion the magic in you. One of the women in my life at that time, Marisa, saw in me more than I saw in myself. Together we relocated from Fort Collins, Colorado, to Jacksonville, Florida, thanks to a timely relocation package offered to her by Merrill Lynch.

With Marisa's support, I leveraged my years in retail management to break into the world of finance. The structure and stability of my new life lessened my work-related distractions and increased my cash flow. The next two years I traveled almost every weekend, escaping the growing heaviness in my heart with shopping, drinking, dancing, and making out. Despite my quest to solve my growing sadness (I journaled, went to therapy, and read *The Artist's Way*), I still couldn't figure out why I felt the way I did. Needing to change things up drastically, I decided to move to New York City. I'm twenty-four years old at this point, and my subconscious was telling me:

"Girl, moving is just geography. Go ahead, distract yourself from having an honest conversation with yourself by taking your same problems to a new ZIP code. This invisible baggage will cost more than your new rent in Long Island."

I moved to New York with $1,500 in my pocket. I had not secured a job and I had no plan. After two weeks I landed a job at Zara in Soho and it only took a month for me to feel bad about being back in an entry-level position. I hit the Internet cafe in Astoria for eight hours straight one day, determined to get a "real" job. Two weeks later I was back in corporate finance making more money than ever before. On one hand, I was thriving in my dream city, a vision I had for myself since I was a teenager. On the other hand, I was excelling in my professional life, which felt like a tightening of the noose while my family boasted and cheered about how proud they were of me for finally finding my "niche."

I didn't make it to my second anniversary in New York before hitting a depth of sadness I had never felt before. At this point, I was on antidepressants that were numbing my emotions in one way, but causing suicidal thoughts to get clearer at the same time. After my third attempt at taking my own life, I learned a lot about our mental health care system.

The emphasis during my healing was put on the cocktail of pills that would stabilize my mood. There was no advice on how to heal the communication within myself, as well as with my family members, to come to a place together as people with PTSD.

Ironically, I ended up back in Denver after a nationwide search to find a program that would help me cognitively heal. I had a fierce dedication to getting off my medications and handling the PTSD I had from the war as well as my father's abandonment and abuse on my own, without the help of medication. It took me two years to get to that point, but I got there and have been there ever since.

By the fall of 2005 I was back in New York and enrolled in college to finish my degree. For the first time in my life I asked myself what I wanted, and my answer wasn't limited by the automatic beliefs. I graduated with honors and a marketing degree in 2008 at the age of thirty amidst a collapsing economy, but I found myself laid off from my dream job in fashion the day before I was supposed to start.

My heart dropped when I got the phone call, and the following two months I struggled with my confidence. The same voices popped up that tried to remind me of "my place" in the world, and told me to play it safe. I began to dive into a business idea that I started to formulate in my first year at LIM College—an organization called Free Your Star Foundation. I wrote curricula for three business-of-fashion programs and set my sights on Brooklyn high schools. I pitched my curriculum, and the next four years I successfully worked with some of the most amazing individuals I have ever met.

Entrepreneurs create businesses to solve problems they see in the world. As an older college student I shared the classroom with those a decade my junior, and it was quickly evident to me that exposure (not just money) is key in helping a kid understand the possibilities for their future. When I actually got into the work of exposing inner-city youth to the possibilities, it was their emotional well-being that would keep them from growing from the fundamentals learned in our fashion programs. The root of their problems would not leave my consciousness, and that's when fashion began to feel fickle. After four years with the Foundation and a decade in New York, I took a year sabbatical in Puerto Rico to revisit my purpose.

I took the time to write my own thesis on the building blocks for change within our communities, starting with the woman's voice, particularly her emotional intelligence and the inner voice that holds her back. I wrote the first draft of my book *Find Your Voice* in 2012 during my year in Puerto Rico and two years later it was published.

Traveling from my new home in Houston to speaking engagements across the nation, I was humbled to speak to folks at Facebook, HBO, and Whole Foods, and be on the same stage as Brené Brown and Jane Goodall. I was even more touched by the people I met who confided in me how my story changed their perspective. The women had so many business ideas with social impact at the core, and the men—they surprised me with their vulnerability on many occasions.

In 2016 I was assaulted, along with the assault on our society by electing a self-admitted sexual predator to the highest leadership role in our country. For nearly two months I didn't go anywhere and barely talked to anyone. Communicating with my mom became the most I could do. I ran my fingers across my journal with embossed letters that read "I'm the Shero of this story" and began to silently nod to myself. I knew the journey to healing would be a bitch and I refused to harbor hate in my heart for men as I embarked on healing this new wound.

The essence of any attack bestowed upon me from a young age to now had to do with his need to regain control and power. From my father, to my former partner, to a person close to me that assaulted me, they were emotionally unintelligent men shown only one way of coping with their fear, anxiety, and depression. Fortunately I chose to embrace the healthy side of my anger and allowed it to feed my voice of courage and clarity. I redirected my focus to my talents as a professional communicator and conscious leader.

I became a personal branding strategist and got behind other voices because I needed hope and courage—in myself and in society at large. I actively became the shero of my story by not watching TV, taking my own advice from Find Your Voice, meditating, doing yoga, talk therapy, attending support groups, and journaling.

At the same time I was creating a personal branding firm, which launched in October 2018 with a day-long conference titled "Own Your Voice Summit." It was intentionally planned on my fortieth birthday as a coat of arms for myself and a call to conscious leaders to scale their voices for social impact. Each speaker was a knight at my round table, helping me sharpen my sword and strengthen my shield for the important work we have to do as leaders across industries.

As my personal life brought me to experience the neglectful justice and mental health systems in our country, I was faced with the same reality I met on the road with Find Your Voice—there are so many impactful voices educated and equipped to make a change; I wanted to find them and scale their voices to make social impact.

The last leg of my journey thus far has been the most challenging. I'm not the only one leading from a place that holds as much joy as it does pain. Many of us who hold leadership positions have experienced trauma and embody a voice shaped by our experiences. This affects not only us and our families, but also our workplace and our communities on such a deep level.

I purposefully chose speakers whose voices would make the audience stop, wonder, and consider adopting a new perspective. I wanted to wake Houston up by having women of various ethnic and professional backgrounds, alongside men, on the same stage to talk about the decision-making habits of conscious leaders at work.

Imagine if your workplace was a place that empowered you to put down the baggage and focus on your mastery instead. Until that is the norm, I ask you to continue to wonder about the power of your own voice and surround yourself with those who champion your growth. If there is one thing I have learned and that I am sure of, it is that every voice has an opportunity to make a positive impact.

MAYA JAFER

EVERY SO OFTEN, A TV SHOW COMES ALONG THAT completely changes the way we think of the world and about people. When *Transparent* debuted on Amazon in 2014, it became a breakthrough show about the lives of transgender individuals—specifically, a parent named Maura, played by Jeffrey Tambor—and for the first time offered visibility to the trans community in a way that was humanizing, flawed, realistic, and nuanced. Among the show's many cast members were real trans folks who played recurring or guest roles, all of whom intersected with Maura and her family. In season 1, an episode titled "The Letting Go" featured a trans woman named Maya Jafer, whose own personal story is a reminder of why we need more trans visibility and awareness of the struggles the transgender community faces worldwide.

Maya grew up in India and today resides in Los Angeles. She has a medical background along with a successful career. But growing up in a small, conservative Indian town, she also had aspirations of becoming an actress, having been star-struck by a number of Bollywood icons in her childhood. Maya has been very open about her story, growing up as a boy and a young man struggling with her identity within a traditional family setting and a community that adhered to strict gender roles. Her story was the subject of a documentary called *Mohammed to Maya*, directed by Jeff Roy, as well as part of the Amazon docuseries *This Is Me*, which showcases the difficulties many transgender people face every day.

As a trans woman, Maya is part of one of the most severely ostracized and marginalized communities around the world today. She has a very interesting, shocking, inspiring, and fun life story to tell.

Tell me about your upbringing in India.

I was born and raised in Madurai, Tamil Nadu. I was born as a boy and I was the middle sibling. I have an older brother and younger sister. My upbringing was very strict and religious—we were Muslim and conservative. My parents would beat me up physically and emotionally abuse me when I was very little, especially when I was playing with my mother's scarves. It was imprinted in my mind that being feminine is wrong. I was naturally very feminine. I just was born in the wrong body. But these are things I realized much later in life.

Because we were an Indian traditional Muslim family, it was about making sure the daughter or sister knows how to cook and clean and be a good housewife, be a good girl, etc., which my sister was none of. She was a typical tomboy. I took it upon me to make her feminine, telling her how to braid her hair. So I lived my femininity through her. Even though I couldn't really say it out loud to myself because of the brainwashing, it was very clear to me that I was a girl, not a boy.

When did you first know you were transgender?

Initially I thought maybe I'm gay because that was my first experience. I was probably fourteen or fifteen at the time. I read in a magazine an article about an actor, Deepak Parashar, and people were talking about how he was gay. In those times it was unacceptable. So that's when I thought, "maybe I am gay," because I was very attracted to guys. Over time, I met a transgender woman, who are considered Hijras in North India. We met on a movie set. Typically most people would be disgusted by her, but I kind of empathized with her. I also met a transgender classical Indian dancer, and that's when I began to realize that that was who I am.

But it was a sad fact because I had seen the plight of the transgender women—they were considered disgusting, they were shunned and

mocked. That's why I kept it hidden for so long. Not only did I come from a strict Muslim area where it was completely unacceptable—where people wouldn't consider such things, let alone say it out loud—society in general was very antigay, antitrans. I was completely against the idea, even though I knew deep inside that is how I felt. It scared the shit out of me that I would be one of *them*.

When did you start coming out to friends and family?

Coming out to my friends and family didn't happen until after I transitioned, which began at the age of thirty-nine, and I started living as a woman at forty, and actually had my gender reassignment surgery at the age of forty-one, in 2011.

When did you first find a trans community you could feel comfortable with being yourself around?

Never in India. I moved to the United States on a student visa to do my second doctorate in natural medicine at the age of thirty in 2000. By 2003 I had made some friends in Seattle, Washington. A few of them were transgender and one of them was a lesbian and she recognized the feminine in me. By this time I knew that I was transgender.

Was there a lot of acceptance for the trans community in 2003, even in Seattle?

Yes. Seattle was very trans positive and even has a larger trans community than any other city outside of California. I made friends with the lesbian and was able to share with her that I'm transgender, but I don't want to do anything about it, I'm too scared. She took me to a transgender support group, which was my first time seeing primarily Caucasian trans women. They were very supportive and nice. I decided that at some point

I'm going to transition. I met with a trans man, we became friends, he supported me. I asked a lot of questions. He also let me know very clearly that it is not an easy thing to do, meaning to transition or even come out as transgender. Because it requires hormone therapy and your life changes in every way.

Even though you grew up having aspirations of being an actor, you ended up studying medicine?

The only way I could be taken seriously or be respected was through education, which I learned very quickly. I went to a school which was known to produce many professional doctors and engineers. When I graduated from there at the age of eighteen, I then got admission into a homeopathic medical college in Tamil Nadu. I desperately wanted to be a doctor because by then it was imprinted in my mind just through my school surroundings, that that was the ticket to a better life, and more respect.

How did you first get recognition from others as a trans woman?

After graduating I was volunteering and teaching in a Buddhist organization which primarily helps poor people, giving them free treatment. The chief guru, from the moment he saw me he recognized the feminine in me, even though I was still living as a man. He gave me the name Maya. Maya is Buddha's mother's name. But of course I never came out or did anything with the name until much later in my life. So that was the first recognition that I got as a woman. He didn't even call me trans, he called me a girl. I never saw myself as "trans," I always saw myself as a girl; I just happened to be trans.

How did the gender reassignment surgery become a turning point in your life?

After I graduated from my second doctorate in natural medicine, I moved to San Francisco for a year, but I didn't really like it. I eventually moved to Los Angeles in 2005. LA was the place for me because aside from being a doctor, my main passion was always to be an actor. As the years went on, my depression became severe and clinical. Although I was working full-time, I felt I was just going through life with no hope. In 2008, when I was thirty-eight, the financial crisis hit, and many people lost their jobs, including me. Now I had a lot more time on my hands to deal with my depression.

I reached a point where I was suicidal. I decided I needed to see a therapist. So I went to the Los Angeles LGBT center, which is one of the largest of its kind in the world. The first day I met my therapist I let her know that I'm transgender. Eventually she convinced me to go and attend a free transgender support group in the same center. It was there that I first started feeling like I was part of a supportive community and could truly and fully be myself as Maya. I didn't have to hide and could voice my struggles and desires to a group of people who were there for me and were able to give me advice, having been on this journey themselves. I felt more seen and heard than ever before. Eventually I found the resources and information to get the gender reassignment surgery, which I decided to get in Thailand. I decided to document the procedure, which ended up being turned into the award-winning film *Mohammed To Maya*, which showcases not just my surgery but how I decided to start sharing my story as a way to break down stigma, especially in India. It was the right decision and the best decision for me, and I feel honored that I can now share my story with the world.

> MY JOURNEY
> IS A TESTAMENT
> ABOUT WHAT CAN
> HAPPEN WHEN
> YOU EMBRACE
> YOUR JOURNEY
> AND
> LEAN IN TO
> THE POWER IT
> MAY HAVE IN
> THE WORLD.

What makes you a powerful woman?

My journey is a testament about what can happen when you embrace your journey and lean in to the power it may have in the world. It took me many years to learn who I truly was, and not be afraid to live my authentic self. I hope my story will empower others to know that despite what they may face, you should never go through life being anything other than who you truly are.

WOMEN
ENTREPRENEURS

IN OCTOBER 2019, AMERICAN ENTREPRENEUR AUDREY Gelman, founder and CEO of women-focused shared workspace business The Wing, appeared on the cover of *Inc.* magazine. It got many people talking because she was the first visibly pregnant CEO to appear on the cover of a business magazine. A number of social media posts praising the cover remarked how this shouldn't have been so revolutionary since it was 2019, but it speaks to a larger shift happening in the entrepreneur world and what women specifically are doing.

In record numbers, women, especially women of color and minority women, are disrupting typical models and ideals of entrepreneurship and making pathways for others like them. According to Inc.com, every day in the United States women start 849 new businesses. Many of these women start their own businesses out of necessity, in part due to limitations for growth in the corporate world.

The 2018 State of Women-Owned Business Report showed that the number of women-owned businesses grew an impressive 58 percent from 2007 to 2018, and more specifically the number of firms owned by black women grew by 164 percent. Black women are the only racial or ethnic group with more business ownership than their male peers, according to the Federal Reserve. These numbers are inspiring, to be sure, but the avenues for funding are still hard to crack. Women are increasingly turning to crowdfunding platforms and other private means of raising the money they need to start their businesses, as opposed to the traditional angel investment or venture capital route that has helped so many male entrepreneurs. These are businesses that cater to their communities in ways the traditional business world has often ignored. Whether it is menstrual hygiene companies that also work to destigmatize the issue with education, helping young low-income women get into the STEM pipeline by learning how to code, or creating technology that addresses sexual harassment in the workplace, women are using entrepreneurship as a way to assert their authority/knowledge/skill/leadership and make the world a less hostile place to live in.

The statistics can only tell you so much of the story. What you need is to see these women up close and hear about their journeys to understand how the world of entrepreneurship and business could be something within reach of your own grasp, if you have the right role models. In this chapter you will get to read about women who are creating a new model of entrepreneurial success.

AMALI DE ALWIS

MEET AMALI DE ALWIS. SHE IS A PIONEER, A CEO, AND an all-round badass in an industry that is accustomed to singing the praises of men on a daily basis. Amali is the CEO of Code First: Girls and was recently named the UK's most influential woman in tech.

Code First: Girls is a multiaward-winning social enterprise working with companies and women to increase the proportions of women in tech, and over the past four years it has delivered 5.4 million+ dollars worth of free tech education, has taught six-thousand-plus women how to code for free, and has helped companies to recruit and train better tech talent in their firms. At the end of 2017, Amali spearheaded a campaign to teach twenty thousand women to code by the end of 2020.

Her organization is credited with teaching more women to code in the UK than British universities do! Their approach to engaging a demographic that is only in recent years being sought out by the tech industry explains why they are having so much success.

Tell us where your interest in coding and computer programming came from.

My first experiences of coding were learning BASIC as a kid, and then I learned Fortran as part of my engineering degree. But my focus wasn't on coding. It was on building things—whether that was sewing a waistcoat for my Barbie doll or making a radio with my electronics set. I didn't mind as long as I was making something and using my creativity.

How did you get involved with Code First: Girls?

I was hired into Code First: Girls (CF:G) as its first CEO in 2015. It had started as a small program in a company called Entrepreneur First (EF). As EF grew and changed direction, they still had lots of interest in the Code First: Girls courses, so they decided to spin off CF:G as an independent company and then brought me in to build the program into a company.

At one point I also became increasingly involved in mentoring. So when I came across the opportunity to head up Code First: Girls as its first CEO, I couldn't say no!

BUT MY FOCUS WASN'T ON CODING. IT WAS ON BUILDING THINGS—WHETHER THAT WAS SEWING A WAISTCOAT FOR MY BARBIE DOLL OR MAKING A RADIO WITH MY ELECTRONICS SET.

CF:G has been training more than the annual number of women studying coding-based subjects across the UK's university system. How did you achieve this?

As someone who is a former quantitative researcher, I always like to look at the data. So when we were trying to understand the tech talent landscape for our 2020 Campaign, we went and pulled the UCAS university undergraduate application datasets. What we found was that for UCAS acceptances in 2017, of the 27,400 individuals who were accepted into a computer science degree, only 3,750 (13.7 percent) were women.

We didn't believe that this was enough, so set ourselves the target to teach twenty thousand young women how to code for free by the end of 2020. And we're well on track. This semester we delivered eighty-five coding courses across the UK and taught around eighteen hundred young women how to code for free. That will be increasing to two thousand to twenty-two hundred next semester, which means we will be teaching around five thousand women how to code for free each year.

Change has to start at the leadership level, and when we look at the CF:G team, we see women and especially women of color. How do you encourage other organizations to look at their leadership team as well as the pipeline of women they serve?

The key is to frame diversity discussions around what that organization needs to grow and thrive. For all our businesses, access to tech talent is an ongoing challenge. And with Brexit soon upon us, we will have to think carefully about how we can continue to nurture a talent pool that can support our organization and enable the UK to remain a global leader in tech and innovation. So encouraging people to look to the future and consider increasing diversity can help support those objectives and become a powerful catalyst.

Do you feel there is an added race component in the barriers to women's success in STEM? And how does culture play a role in sometimes holding women of color back?

Ethnicity and culture, and the intersectionality between them and gender, play a complicated role in career progression—especially when it comes to whether people believe tech careers are suitable for themselves or for others. Unconscious bias does play a role, as does self-selection of career path based on what we grow up with seeing as "normal" or to be expected. It's why it's so important that the public narrative we have on tech includes people from diverse backgrounds, as it's the only way that we can reposition what we expect as "normal" in tech.

Who are some women in STEM you personally admire?

Jude Milhon, who was a hacker and author, civil rights activist, and coined the term "cypherpunk." Marian R. Croak, a pioneer in Internet telephony and VOIP technology who holds over three hundred and fifty patents. Radia Perlman, who was an early pioneer of the Internet and created the spanning tree protocol, which is a network protocol that helps avoid looping issues in Ethernet network—critical for the broadcast industry.

Lixia Zhang is a professor of computer science at the University of California who was one of the twenty-one participants in the initial meeting of the Internet Engineering Task Force (where the first standards for the Internet were created) in 1986, and the only woman and the only student at the meeting.

What makes you a powerful woman?

The power I have is around the ability to influence. Through Code First: Girls we've been able to build a powerful voice of change for the tech industry, and create a common narrative where others who want to access a tech career, or encourage others from diverse backgrounds to be able to do so, can come together and drive change together. This is about helping women access exciting, well-paid careers. I think that's pretty powerful stuff!

UMAIMAH MENDHRO

UMAIMAH MENDHRO IS THE FOUNDER AND
CEO OF VIDA, AN E-COMMERCE COMPANY
THAT COMBINES MINDFUL GLOBAL CITIZENSHIP
AND STYLE THROUGH CAREFULLY SELECTED
ARTISTIC PARTNERSHIPS AND RESPONSIBLY
SOURCED, BEAUTIFUL PRODUCTS THAT CONNECT
DESIGNERS, PRODUCERS, AND CONSUMERS.

THAT'S JUST THE TIP OF THE ICEBERG WHEN IT
COMES TO UMAIMAH'S EMPOWERING STORY AND
HER INCREDIBLE CAREER PATH IN SILICON VALLEY.
UMAIMAH WAS BORN IN PAKISTAN AND LIVED
IN A RURAL VILLAGE BEFORE HER FAMILY LEFT
TO LIVE IN EXILE IN SAUDI ARABIA AND THE UK,
EVENTUALLY MOVING BACK HOME. HER PARENTS,
BOTH DOCTORS (HER DAD WAS THE FIRST IN
HIS FAMILY TO GO TO COLLEGE, AND HER MOM
BUILT A HOSPITAL), WERE VERY POLITICALLY AND
SOCIALLY ACTIVE DURING HER UPBRINGING.

THEY WERE FRIENDS WITH FORMER PAKISTANI PRIME Minister Benazir Bhutto, the first woman to head a democratic government in a Muslim majority nation. Umaimah recalls meeting Benazir and being inspired by her, as she was pregnant while running for office. Growing up being surrounded by people, especially women, who were anomalies among the rest of the Pakistani community, became the starting point for her passion to want to make a difference in the world.

"I always knew I wanted to build something and make my life matter," she told me in an interview.

Her maternal grandfather believed in education for his daughters as well as his son, and was adamant they would have the same opportunities as boys. Because she was born into this forward-thinking environment, she had the ability to dream big about her future and know there was life beyond her immediate surroundings.

"I used to daydream about being either the prime minister of Pakistan or a CEO," she recalls.

While the former has not eventuated (yet!), it was the latter aspiration that came into being because she had the chance to study. Umaimah earned a BS from Cornell University in human development with coursework in computer science and eventually earned an MBA from Harvard Business School. She began her career by working at major tech companies like Microsoft, where, as the Director of Product, she led the division's efforts around incubation on Xbox Kinect.

Her resume is full of startup and tech experience for multi-million-dollar businesses, managing growth strategies for some of the most sought-after companies, and working with game-changing companies in the pre-IPO stage. But it would be a trip back to her home country that sparked the idea for VIDA. She wanted to create a platform that brought together designers and creators, and take out the "middle man."

"These two worlds are generally so far apart in fashion and design, but they don't have to be," she said. "The fashion industry is dictated by buyers and trend forecasters. I wanted to find out whether it was

possible to use technology to turn that model on its head."

In Pakistan, she spent a lot of time in factories learning about how the work gets done and about the lives of those creating the product. It bothered her to see how the system where all the money went to those at the top meant cycles of poverty continued, and she didn't think that was fair. She wanted to create a way to empower workers to make more money without it having to be a charity, as such.

"VIDA makes the whole ecosystem more efficient, as there are no huge markups, the factory workers earn more, and it becomes a sustainable model," she said.

The idea was formed, and the only thing left to get it off the ground was seed funding. Thanks to connections she made at Harvard, she presented the idea to investors at Google Ventures, and secured funding on her first pitch. This is not something to gloss over, especially when it comes to the systemic sexism that exists in the tech world.

According to TechCrunch, women-founded companies are still not being funded at anywhere near an equal rate as male-founded ones. But as the *Harvard Business Review* points out, studies show many female-founded companies have a higher rate of return on average than their male counterparts. And with only 8 percent of venture capital firms in the United States having female partners, there is a need for more women making the funding decisions as well. Umaimah says sexism has been a problem in Silicon Valley for a long time; it's just that the stories are finally coming to light now.

"The conversations we're having right now about the need for more diversity can be uncomfortable and awkward, but they are necessary. I am hopeful it will get better and lead to change," she said.

Along with her career success, Umaimah never lost sight of her desire to make a difference in the world. She founded an organization called Dreamfly, which is a global initiative connecting communities in conflict around common causes, with a presence across four countries touching over five thousand lives. Dreamfly kick-starts seed initiatives that are 100 percent financially sustainable within one year. Wanting to help people in Pakistan escape the cycle of poverty was also buoyed by a major historical event.

"Post September 11 [2001], I wanted to reframe people's idea of Pakistan, by sharing the stories of kids' lives," she said.

The idea has since expanded to Afghanistan, Rwanda, and India, where people in poverty create projects that become a self-sustaining source of income. Umaimah is the kind of role model who understands that not everyone is born with the same opportunities in life to get ahead, but that those who do have advantages like her can use that to empower others and lift them out of poverty. In the factories where the VIDA products are made, they have introduced literacy programs for the workers, which have in turn opened up even more opportunities and possibilities for their children.

It's important to know that each of us has the potential to do great things with what we are given. When I asked Umaimah how she would define "power," she said perseverance.

"It can be a self-fulfilling prophecy. If you genuinely believe you will persevere, you will. There is strength and power in perseverance," she said.

THE CONVERSATIONS WE'RE HAVING RIGHT NOW ABOUT THE NEED FOR MORE DIVERSITY CAN BE UNCOMFORTABLE AND AWKWARD, BUT THEY ARE NECESSARY.

CHEF ALINA Z

MEET CHEF ALINA Z—AN INSPIRING CHEF, AUTHOR, AND host of a podcast called *Hungry for Miracles,* focusing on miraculous stories from everyday women. Her mission is to teach people, especially women, that eating healthy can taste good and that it all starts with self-love.

Chef Alina is the creator of the #1 Best Diet (2015), an organic plant-based detox, as voted by *Harper's Bazaar* magazine. She is a health coach and private chef, specializing in the psychology behind eating and how to create healthy and largely plant-based cuisine, which she details in her book, *Single & Hungry: A Realistic Guide to Food & Self-Love.*

She also has an incredible story of overcoming adversity and even *choosing* adversity. She came from a very poor Russian family that eventually became the wealthiest family in St. Petersburg. At age fifteen, she chose to leave a life of luxury to set out and make it on her own in America. Her family business went bankrupt and she had to build herself from the bottom up.

Can you tell me about your upbringing in Russia?

When I was born, we were very poor. Then, in 1988, my parents had an idea for a business—a sewing company—and won an American grant to start it. They continued growing the company, and we had

forty-seven different businesses at one point. I saw our lives change and got to travel a lot, visiting many countries in Europe, and even came to the USA a few times, which was rare for the early nineties in Russia. I got to see that there is a different life outside Russia, and it is possible to live your dreams if you dare to follow them.

You came to the United States at age fifteen, and have never looked back. Tell me about that process.

I wanted to create my own life and have people love me for me, not be seen as my parents' daughter who would inherit the businesses. So I researched schools and applied to a boarding school in Maryland. I did everything myself, because my parents didn't speak English. I did my interviews over the phone and via fax! I got accepted, bought a ticket, and came to study with a dream to stay.

A year later, my mom decided to follow me and left our businesses behind to follow her own passion of painting. Of course it was hard in the beginning to adjust to American life, learn the language better, and find my own voice. I remember once my thesis class professor at Parsons School of Design told me I would never get an A in her class because English wasn't my first language. I was about to give up working hard because I didn't see the point. But my mom told me to not pay attention and just focus on my class work. Even though the teacher gave me a C and a B for each semester, I won first place in the entire department against all thesis presentations! I didn't let that teacher hold me back, although I saw that one opinion can sometimes hold us from believing in ourselves.

You are passionate about health and good nutrition. Where does this focus come from?

I used to be addicted to sugar. I had irritable bowel syndrome and acid reflux. I was always tired and needed a solution besides taking medications. I started reading books and learning about health and how to eat better. I would share it with my friends and they saw results too. I loved how it felt to teach and see people get happier and healthier, so I quit my nine-to-five marketing job and turned my newfound passion into a career.

Your work has become a go-to source for billionaires, celebrities, and famous athletes. What has that experience been like?

It was one of the most humbling experiences to see a celebrity in her casual clothes at home, without any makeup on and with a big smile on her face because I was making her healing food. I also find that when I support influencers and people who change lives, I get to be a part of their work as well. When I support them with good food, they can inspire and help more people live better lives. I feel honored that my clients see the value in what I do.

Diets and nutrition can be very intimidating and overwhelming. Your approach is to find a plan that fits the individual, similar to the way you find an outfit that suits your body. Can you talk about how you help people find their nutritional "fit"?

We dress according to the weather, our moods, tastes, current fashion, and our body types. Yet, when it comes to food, many people follow a one-size-fits-all diet. I wanted to show people how using fashion as an example, you can find your own style with food. For example, if it's hot outside, you will want to eat something cooling, and if it's cold outside, no matter how good-for-you green smoothies may be, it probably won't be the best choice. I wrote a whole section in the book that I dedicated to food according to fashion.

SELF-LOVE IS THE ONLY THING THAT WILL MAKE HEALTHY EATING A LIFELONG LOVE AFFAIR.

Why do you believe healthy nutrition is an essential part of self-love?

If you eat healthy because you hate yourself and eat to change your body out of spite, it will be short-lived and unpleasant. And where is the fun in that? However, when you love yourself and your body, you want to enjoy life, you want to bring pleasure into your life, you want to take care of you. Self-love is the only thing that will make healthy eating a lifelong love affair.

Finally, what makes you a powerful woman?

My passion, love, and perseverance. When you are passionate, you are ignited; when you love, you are connected; and when you have perseverance, you keep that passion and love moves you.

YASMINE MUSTAFA

ONE OF THE MOST POWERFUL SOCIAL MOVEMENTS we have seen over the past few years is the #MeToo movement, first launched by activist Tarana Burke in 2006 to raise awareness of the pervasiveness of sexual abuse and assault in society. The phrase developed into a broader movement, following the 2017 use of #MeToo as a hashtag after the explosive Harvey Weinstein sexual abuse allegations, amplified by major celebrities and public personalities. We are at a point in history where we are seeing a long-awaited reckoning of the consequences of gender inequality, but it will take constant action and grassroots movement-building in a number of industries, and it certainly won't happen overnight. When a coalition of female Hollywood stars banded together to create the #TimesUp movement to oust powerful men with histories of sexual abuse from their position of authority, what they also did was focus on industries that often get overlooked, such as agriculture and hospitality.

But it's not just celebrities or spokespeople that are helping to push for change. There are companies in the private sector that are recognizing the power they have in tackling the issue in very innovative ways.

One company that is aiming to make an impact is ROAR for Good, a Philadelphia-based women's safety wearable tech company who released their first product in 2015, called Athena. The founder

of the company is Yasmine Mustafa, who combines her background and her personal experiences from around the world with her passion to make a difference for women when it comes to sexual assault in the workplace and beyond.

Tell us in a nutshell what ROAR for Good does.

The company was created to empower women to live their lives boldly and without fear. We're a social impact B-corp developing safety jewelry for women and investing part of the proceeds in educational programs that combat violence.

Our first product is called Athena, after the Greek goddess of courage and wisdom. It's a piece of jewelry that can be worn as a necklace, clipped to clothing, or attached to a key fob. It has a button on it that can be pressed whenever the wearer feels threatened. Once activated, it emits a loud alarm to deter attackers and sends text messages to family and friends with their current location. We are also working on a solution to enable it to automatically call 911 or an emergency number.

How did you come up with the idea for Athena?

First, I traveled across South America by myself for six months. Everywhere I stayed, I met women who had been assaulted. A week after I returned, a woman was brutally raped a block from my apartment. Everything hit home at once when I read the news story, and that's when the idea was born. Initially, I thought about what women use to protect themselves and realized the biggest weakness of self-defense tools were that you had to pull them out of your pocket or purse. So I thought, why not make them wearable so they're easily accessible. The first product was going to be called the "Macelet"—mace in a bracelet.

I put a survey together and shared it with everyone I knew. I learned it was actually a terrible idea. That women didn't like existing solutions like pepper spray, Tasers, and knives because they were too aggressive, they felt intimidated by them, and, most significantly, they were afraid they would be overpowered and their own device would be used against them. I went back to the drawing board to design something that is safe to the wearer, and thus Athena was born.

You have traveled solo across the world. Where did you go and what was the most startling thing you learned?

I started in Ecuador and did a four-week Spanish immersion program. From there, I went to Colombia, Argentina, Chile, Bolivia, and Peru, spending about a month in each country. The trip was life-changing. I faced some internal struggles, I put myself out of my comfort zone by going to new places, eating different food, and meeting new people every day.

One of the most startling aspects of the trip is realizing how prevalent attacks against women are, with both locals and travelers alike.

> I SHOULD HAVE HAD A DIFFERENT LIFE WITH LIMITED OPPORTUNITIES, BUT I DIDN'T, AND I REALIZE HOW LUCKY I AM.

Why is raising awareness about domestic violence and gender violence so important to you?

While I was born in Kuwait, my family was whisked away when I was eight years old during the Persian Gulf War. I feel like I cheated the "birth lottery." I should have had a different life with limited opportunities, but I didn't, and I realize how lucky I am. I follow the injustice of how women are treated in other countries and have had a lifelong passion for championing the underserved.

As I started digging into the statistics—one in three women have experienced dating violence or domestic abuse, one in four college females will be sexually assaulted, one in five women have experienced rape or attempted rape—I became horrified at the epidemic of violence against women. As a technologist, I wanted to do something to help that had a lasting impact.

Originally the Athena was marketed to address the sexual assault problem happening on college campuses across the United States. Now your company's new mission is to create safer work environments. Why did you pivot your focus toward the hospitality industry?

A recent survey found 58 percent of housekeepers have experienced sexual harassment. The majority are women of color or immigrants. English is their second language. They're groped in the hotel room, solicited for sex acts, or worse. Every day they go to work, they put themselves at risk. The power dynamic between the male guest that can afford to stay there and the person cleaning the room creates an environment that makes this type of harassment commonplace.

Thankfully, legislation started to pass requiring hotels to protect their staff—including supplying them with panic buttons. With AlwaysOn, our hotel employee safety platform, we can help protect people in the workplace, and foster confidence.

I have experienced firsthand the harassment and feelings of powerlessness many of these women face when I was undocumented. No one should be afraid while trying to earn a wage.

How does the Athena help housekeepers when they are in an unsafe situation?

In an uncomfortable or emergency situation, a housekeeper will press the safety wearable and our platform will automatically triangulate her location and send security personnel or the first responder with her exact location.

We took great care to build a reliable platform that will give peace of mind and emotional security so staff members truly feel empowered. We created our system with the same mission-critical systems used in banking, and reinforced it to work without Wi-Fi, cell, or power so there's multiple backup systems and no single point of failure.

Why do you think it is important to see issues primarily faced by women being addressed by innovation?

Women encompass half the planet and make the majority of purchasing decisions for their families, yet men lead most of the innovation. This creates a disconnect between those who are making the technology and those consuming it. It's important to have women innovate, as it provides the opportunity to tap into their own pain points. This increases the likelihood of developing a better product or solution as a result. Just look at the advancements in breast pumps, period underwear, pregnancy tests, and of course, our own safety solution.

Did you experience any pushback from investors when trying to raise money for Athena?

I have not raised money using the traditional VC (venture capital) route yet. I have pitched to investors and experienced a few unfortunate incidents. I've been called "little lady" or had investors look to my male cofounder at the time for answers while I was sitting right next to them. In one meeting I had stepped out to use the restroom when one of the investors turned to my male cofounder and said he would invest if HE was running the company. The last stat I read said only approximately 2 percent of VC money goes to female founders. But I've seen a surge of women- and minority-led funds in the last year. I also believe we need more women as VCs to help as well.

[Yasmine Mustafa ended up successfully raising money for Athena through an Indiegogo crowdfunding campaign instead.]

As a former refugee, having traveled to America and learning you were undocumented when applying for college, how has your own experience shaped the work you do today?

I have experienced the fear, uncertainty, language barriers, culture shock, workplace discrimination, and the feeling of not belonging when trying to make a place for myself in this country. Those experiences fueled my passion to become a social entrepreneur and help the underserved. This vision inspired the launch of ROAR for Good, which leverages technology to create safer environments for women.

What makes you a powerful woman?

As someone who grew up as a minority in my neighborhood and spent a decade undocumented, I had big dreams of what I would do once I had the freedom to choose my own path. Hopefully my story inspires others in the same situation, as inspiration is powerful.

SUZANNE SIEMENS & MADELEINE SHAW

OVER THE PAST FEW YEARS A LOT OF PROGRESS HAS been made in the movement to end social and cultural stigma around menstruation. In a number of developing countries, when a girl gets her period, she is often forced to stay home and miss school. This compounds over the years and affects her ability to gain an education and in turn be financially stable. Some girls don't have access to sanitary menstrual hygiene products and use items such as sticks or rags. In extreme cases, we've seen cultures that banish girls and menstruating women from participating in religious ceremonies or daily family activities, and some are banished from the house altogether.

In the developed world, stigma presents itself in different ways: menstrual hygiene products being taxed as a "luxury" item, incarcerated women being denied access to sanitary products, and media portrayal of a normal bodily function as something "gross." But we are also seeing some incredible activism and pushback to the stigma in a number of ways—whether it is musician and activist Kian Gandhi "free bleeding" during a marathon to raise awareness about menstrual stigma, organizations successfully lobbying to end the "tampon tax" in countries like Canada, or, more recently, the Academy Award–winning documentary *Period. End of Sentence,* which drew attention to this global problem.

There are also for-profit brands and businesses affecting change. Lunapads is a Canadian-based company that produces menstrual hygiene products, but also utilizes brand awareness to educate consumers about menstrual stigma and the importance of sexual health. Founders Suzanne Siemens and Madeleine Shaw consider themselves the OGs of alternative menstrual products and period activism, and their work speaks for itself. Along with their product range, they also have a couple of programs where they partner with NGOs in the developing world to provide menstrual products to people who don't have easy access.

Their goal is to change the game and do away with the shame around menstruation.

The main goal of Lunapads is for customers to have a more "informed experience" of their bodies. How does menstrual stigma lead to lack of information?

When we're afraid or ashamed of something, it makes it harder to ask questions or to get help. It can be risky to talk openly about periods. Consequences can include being shamed, criticized, or denied. In some cultures, periods signal sexual readiness or marriageability. When we have a more informed experience about our periods we naturally develop a more positive relationship with our bodies. Periods can feel embarrassing, inconvenient, and painful. But recognizing that periods should be a normal part of our body experience allows us to be more accepting and curious, seek help, or simply feel better about ourselves and our bodies.

You both met at a leadership conference and decided to launch this company together. Why did you decide on tackling menstrual stigma?

Suzanne had been struggling with fertility and multiple miscarriages for several years, so she was seeking ways to be gentler with and more supportive of her reproductive health.

Madeleine had been thinking about period politics and experimenting with making and selling washable pads and period

Suzanne Siemens (left) and Madeleine Shaw (right)

underwear for a few years, but lacked business experience. She too had had her own health issues related to tampons, and was frustrated with the wastefulness of disposable products.

Our thoughts converged around values: selling reusable products with an explicit pro-period, shame-free message, and telling customers that we were about creating social change through progressive product choices and business practices. Lunapads' original tagline was "Your Body. Your World. Your Choice."

Was the philanthropic/activist aspect always part of what you envisioned?

Lunapads was definitely an activist brand right out of the gate. We donated products to local women's shelters as early as 1995, and continue to do so today. We started working with marginalized menstruators in Global South nations in 2000, and became a Founding Canadian B Corporation in 2012.

Thanks to being actively involved in the B Corp community, we are constantly finding new ways to make a positive and sustainable impact to prove that business can be a powerful force for social change.

Tell us about Pads4Girls and One4Her, and how empowering girls in the developing world has a direct correlation with their level of education and financial stability.

There is a direct correlation between personal health and hygiene, access to education, and personal empowerment. Without access to clean water, private toilets, and access to supplies to help them manage their periods, girls will miss days and weeks of school every year. Educating a girl is the most powerful way to help lift families out of poverty.

When we understood this correlation, we began Pads4Girls and One4Her as a way to support and raise awareness of this issue. It began in the year 2000 with sending pad donations to countries in the Global South. Then in 2008 we were approached by two North American development workers in Uganda who asked us for permission to copy the Lunapads model of making washable pads. Today, we continue to support AFRIpads in their business, which employs over two hundred local Ugandans and has served over three million girls with menstrual pads.

Can you each share with us a particular story that touched you personally?

MADELEINE: Going to Uganda in 2012 and meeting the AFRIpads team and visiting their factory (AFRIpads opened a brand-new 8,000-square-foot modern factory in June 2019). At the time, they had a staff of around twenty-five women and were using foot-powered sewing machines to make the pads. I tried my hand at it and had this overwhelming moment of imagining myself almost twenty years earlier, sewing Lunapads back in Vancouver. I never could have dreamed that it would take me as far as Uganda.

SUZANNE: Our trip to Uganda was the number one highlight for me too. I was also very touched by a story from a girl in Ethiopia. Saba told us that because she now had our cloth pads to help her manage her period, she was able to convince her parents that she should stay in school and not be married off as a young girl. Today, she is a high school graduate with a promising future ahead of her.

What do you think is the root cause of people thinking menstruation and women's bodies are "gross"?

It comes down to a primal fear of the unknown and things that can't be completely understood, controlled, or dominated. Everything to do with giving life—sensuality, fecundity, bodies, blood, milk, sex, even beauty—can be something that people feel the need to take down or desecrate.

EDUCATING A GIRL IS THE MOST POWERFUL WAY TO HELP LIFT FAMILIES OUT OF POVERTY.

It's basically impossible for anyone not to hold some form of internalized body shame. This is especially true for women, trans and nonbinary individuals, and especially for those with periods. We are hardwired to want to belong and feel included. So when someone is "grossed out" by the idea of reusable menstrual products, it can be a reflection of that pervasive social conditioning. Most of us have been conditioned to believe it's taboo, dirty, painful, and inconvenient, rather than framed as a marker of health and fertility.

You have also placed a focus on being environmentally conscious by helping to divert disposable tampons or pads away from landfills in North America. Can you share more about this?

Each year, over twenty billion pads, tampons, and applicators end up in North American landfills and oceans. Over their lifetime, the average menstruator will use twelve thousand pads/tampons, throw away three hundred pounds of waste, and spend three thousand dollars on menstrual supplies. But thanks to customers using our products, we help divert twenty million pads and tampons from landfills every year. We also have a zero-waste manufacturing process and have diverted over thirty-five hundred pounds of textile waste from landfills.

Finally, what makes you both powerful women?

MADELEINE: I believe in possibility and the power of people—especially those whose voices have traditionally been marginalized—to make the world a better place.

It's time for women to take our rightful place in society and to use business as a way to heal and regenerate our communities. We have the tools. We just need the will, courage, and strength to challenge the norms. Knowing this makes me feel empowered and confident in moving forward and making a difference for the future.

SUZANNE: As a girl, I was conditioned to believe I didn't have a voice: it was considered more appropriate to stay quiet and follow the rules. Today, I feel powerful when I can use my voice to support and advance the issues and people I care about. We can't afford to stay quiet anymore. We need to share positive messages not just to our customers but to anyone in our community. It's time to show up and be loud and proud, without caring what others think about you.

MARY PRYOR

ONE OF THE FASTEST-GROWING CHANGES WE'RE SEEING in the United States today is the legalization of cannabis and subsequent cultural attitudes. As of April 2019, eleven states have fully legalized the use of cannabis while in sixteen states it is fully illegal. The other have a mixture of laws relating to decriminalization and medicinal and recreational uses.

Along with the change has come an entrepreneurship boom in the cannabis industry, and most notably with female-founded companies. Because of this fast-growing new sector that hasn't seen a traditional male-dominated power structure like other industries, there are reports stating how women in cannabis are breaking the "grass ceiling."

One of these founders and entrepreneurs is Mary Pryor, cofounder of Cannaclusive, along with partners Tonya Flash and Charlese Antoinette. Launched in July 2017, the consulting and advocacy firm was created to facilitate fair representation of minority cannabis consumers through branding, technology, marketing campaigns, and education. The founding team was inspired by the growing opportunities in this industry but disappointed by the lack of diversity taking root in mainstream cannabis culture. Cannaclusive is helping brands create new narratives, spark dynamic conversations and experiences among customers, and encourage media entities to look beyond the status quo. Mary's own health struggles with Crohn's disease led her to cannabis initially, and now she is utilizing her personal story and entrepreneurship to benefit others. By centering a lot of their focus on people of color, Mary and the Cannaclusive team are working to shift culture by amplifying the voices and lives of marginalized people in this industry.

Tell us about your first experience with marijuana and using it to manage pain from Crohn's disease.

It came out of a moment of desperation. I didn't have access to pain medication while on a trip and I ended up visiting a dispensary while on a camping excursion in Denver. I bought a recommended strain of White Widow and my pain level decreased to where I could breathe and rest. I would have ended up having a flare-up if I didn't connect those dots that day. This was in the fall of 2014.

When did you start becoming interested in the greater cultural and political conversations around legalizing cannabis?

Summer 2017 in Los Angeles, when I realized that my own experiences as a black woman who tried to find work in the space was met with dismissal and disregard for my experience. I have encountered these types of micro-aggressions throughout my life growing up in Detroit and living in various cities before. But with cannabis it felt personal. I knew that we had been left out due to capital and access before, but those one-on-one moments hit hard.

One of the turning points on the road to creating Cannaclusive was seeing the lack of diverse representation at cannabis events. Can you talk more about this and how you met your cofounders?

Tonya and I met at music events where Mickey Factz, Teyana Taylor, and Billionaire Boys Club were a thing almost ten years ago. Charlese and I met and knew each other from the nightlife scene where she was working as a wardrobe stylist around the same time.

Charlese Antoinette, Mary Pryor, Tonya Rapley-Flash (left to right)

I worked in music and events throughout that period and we always saw each other somewhere out in those New York City streets. We all ended up in Los Angeles due to our shifting careers and started attending cannabis events, which were WOEFULLY lacking in inclusion and diversity. We were often three out of six black and/or brown bodies at a cannabis event. It was a nonstop reminder of the loss and risk of the culture being whitewashed when it comes to understanding multicultural audiences. Women, especially black women, are under-represented in the industry. Driving our importance and value is crucial.

You host a lot of discussion panels and information sessions around the country. What are some of the consistent themes you hear from attendees?

How do you start? Where do you start? Where is the money? How can I get in? What are the opportunities? Is this legal in my state? How do I get a medical marijuana card? How does this help with my health issues? People are hungry, especially in the black and brown communities. People are seeking answers and really need authentic guidance.

How do you hope Cannaclusive can play a role in dismantling the harmful laws put in place surrounding cannabis use?

African American people have been heavily incarcerated for cannabis use and still remain behind bars today disproportionately. We're adapting how we can support our community, implore businesses to encourage and drive forward with social equity programming, reinforce the importance of civic engagement, and teach people about the pitfalls of a noninclusive industry.

PEOPLE ARE HUNGRY, ESPECIALLY IN THE BLACK AND BROWN COMMUNITIES. PEOPLE ARE SEEKING ANSWERS AND REALLY NEED AUTHENTIC GUIDANCE.

Where do you see this issue ten years from now?

Cannabis is already a global conversation. I am concerned with shifting the current climate so that marginalized citizens are no longer called marginalized. There is a global multicultural mass that cannot be ignored and we need access and must plant ourselves into this industry.

Finally, what makes you a powerful woman?

The fact that given all that I've witnessed as a black woman who thrives and manages a chronic illness—that I am still here.

ADISYN PYLES & JIAYI

ACCORDING TO FIGURES FROM UNICEF, HUMAN TRAFFICKING is the second-largest criminal industry in the world, reaping an estimated thirty-two billion dollars in the trade of human beings. Trafficking is considered a form of modern-day slavery that subjects primarily women and girls (an estimated 75 percent of trafficking victims), but also men and boys, to commercial sexual exploitation or forced labor. It is easy to get overwhelmed and feel like there is nothing you can do to stop this injustice. But change begins with one person—or in the case of jewelry and design company Freeleaf, two people. Adisyn Pyles, who hails from the United States, and JiaYi, her business partner who hails from Asia, are the founders of a business that employs victims of the trafficking trade and restores their purpose and beauty, while also enabling them to become financially independent, reducing the likelihood of a survivor being exploited again in the future.

Both of these women decided that waiting around for a superhero to save the day wasn't an option, and instead used their own unique life experiences to make a path forward for vulnerable women and girls throughout Asia, a region that sees some of the highest rates of trafficking in the world. After college, Adisyn spent a gap year in Asia, intending to go back home and eventually apply for grad school. Her ambition had always been to work in the social and nonprofit world, specifically in French-speaking African countries. But her gap year

Adisyn Pyles (left) and JiaYi (right)

turned out to be the turning point in her life, and she has remained there ever since. It was during this time that she met JiaYi, learned about her story of being unwanted by her family for being born a girl, and realized there was an opportunity to work together to help other women and girls who face barriers and become vulnerable to exploitation because of their gender.

They are changing the lives of women, with gender equality as one of their key secret weapons, and a company whose stylish products were created to honor a traditional and ancient Asian art form.

Adisyn, how did you initially create Freeleaf?

I never thought of myself as an entrepreneur, and I definitely never imagined myself moving to the other side of the world to start a fashion and home decor company! Ultimately, my belief that women are made for more was my inspiration. When JiaYi and I started talking in 2015, we both knew that we were passionate about helping women find freedom from abuse and exploitation. Neither of us had any idea how to do that, so we started by listening.

We talked to women from a variety of backgrounds—homeless women, women with mental or physical disabilities, women who have been in the sex industry, domestic abuse survivors, women with low education, trafficking survivors, single moms, and sexual assault survivors. As we listened to women tell their stories, we saw that they were incredibly resilient and capable, but two of the main reasons they remained trapped in abuse were economic need and a lack of viable opportunities. If women were to be able to truly thrive in independent and sustainable lives, they needed a job with fair wages and fair working conditions. This was where the idea of Freeleaf began.

What was it about meeting JiaYi and her story that made you realize the potential in a business like this?

As an American living abroad, the idea of starting a company and stepping into really complex situations of trauma and abuse was overwhelming. I knew that anything I started would only be successful if I had a local partner who was as passionate as I was. I needed someone who would tell me when my ideas were terrible and when my cultural lens was irrelevant or even harmful. I needed someone with both boldness to lead a company and tenderness to walk alongside women in their pain—JiaYi is all of that and more.

JiaYi, can you tell me how gender expectations played a role in how you were brought up?

It was no secret that my parents wanted my sister and me to be born boys. Boys were the ones who carried on the family name and inherited the family's valuables, while girls were only destined to leave and get married. Because of this, families invested more in boys than girls—giving them more opportunities for education and success.

When I was five, I was sent to be raised by my grandparents in the village while my parents worked in the city. I could feel my family's shame at having two daughters, and I hated the feeling of being looked down on. As I grew up, I saw so many of my female peers drop out of school so they could go to work and send their parents money—oftentimes so their brother could go to school and save money to pay his future dowry. I then decided I would study and work hard so I could leave the village and be successful. I needed to prove that as a woman, I could be someone worth being proud of.

Because girls are often seen as less valuable in our society, we have fewer opportunities and are told that we are weaker than men. But I want every woman to see that they have incredible value and potential. I believe women are the key to changing the next generation, and seeing change is something I am passionate about.

Can you explain how Freeleaf works toward solutions to the lack of economic opportunities for trafficking victims?

From the very beginning we saw that economic need and a lack of viable options kept women vulnerable and/or trapped in exploitation. Certain factors like low education, PTSD from previous trauma, schedule challenges of being a single mom, societal pressures, and disabilities can make it challenging for women to find work and be successful. These women don't want handouts or pity—they want opportunities and sustainability. This is why Freeleaf starts with the foundation of providing full-time employment with a fair wage, fair working conditions, and opportunities for upward mobility in the company and vocational training they could take elsewhere if/when they leave.

Can you tell me about the products that are available for purchase through Freeleaf, and what knotting is?

We make a variety of neutral and funky home décor and jewelry/accessory items. All of our products are hand-knotted from a single strand of rope or cord. We drew inspiration from the ancient art form of knotting. All over the world, and especially in Asia, knots have been a symbol of elegance and blessing. We wanted to take elements of this rich traditional culture and bring it into modern applications.

One of our products takes over two hundred feet of rope to make! It's only through patience and dedication that this single strand of rope can be twisted into a stunning piece of art. This process and our products are a constant reminder that even the messiness and confusion of our lives can be woven together to create something incredible. The play on words to creating a world where women are (k)not for sale is just extra.

Can you share any stories from the women you've helped that have impacted you?

The woman who would later become our first staff member in 2015 now says that when we met her, she was at her most depressed and lowest moment with no idea what she was going to do in the future. Together, we fumbled through learning how to make our first product, which was the jute oval rug. Quickly, we realized that she was far better than either of us at creating beauty with her hands.

Over the last three years, she has been able to develop both her artistry and her management skills and she is now Freeleaf's production manager and primary designer. We've seen her become a mom and make incredibly brave choices to set healthy boundaries and leave environments of abuse. She frequently shares her story to encourage all of our new staff in their journey. By walking alongside her as a staff and as a friend, we have come to believe in our mission even more than I did when we started!

THESE WOMEN DON'T WANT HANDOUTS OR PITY— THEY WANT OPPORTUNITIES AND SUSTAINABILITY.

Almost all of our staff are single moms, and by giving them opportunities, we are helping to break cycles of both poverty and abuse. Kofi Annan said it best when he said, "There is no tool for development more effective than the empowerment of women and girls." We absolutely believe this to be true.

How does gender equality play a role in the work you do and your passion for helping these women?

The truth is that women all around the world—from Asia to America—have fewer opportunities and far greater vulnerabilities than men. Women's bodies are constantly policed and we are told both openly and subliminally that we are either "less than" or "too much." The WHO estimates that about one in three women worldwide have experienced physical and/or sexual violence in their lifetime. While we know the two of us and our company aren't capable of solving the world's problems, we also know that we can actively stand and speak against inequality in both our personal and professional lives, and that is a beautiful act of resistance.

What do you think is the root cause of exploitation, and what do you think will be the catalyst to ending it?

Exploitation is such a complex and nuanced issue, and everyone's experience of exploitation or abuse is both unique and layered. It happens on both a systemic and individual level. I think one of the roots of exploitation is believing that people are objects to be used, abused, or ignored rather than actively honoring the innate value of every individual—even those who are so different than you.

There are so many complicated things that need to happen if we're ever to end exploitation. If everyone was willing to step out of their comfort zone to truly listen to and honor those around them, we would surely see a drastic decrease in both individual and systemic abuse.

Finally, what makes you both powerful women?

ADISYN: The first thing that comes to mind is my deep belief that I was made in the image of God. Honoring that gives me the ability to hold the tension of the both/ands of life. As a woman, I can be both strong AND tender, honor the reality of trauma AND still see glimpses of hope, build a successful company AND cherish cuddling my son, be a woman of faith AND question things I've been taught, be a feminist AND love being a wife. I am free to honor the breadth of the human experience both in myself and in others. That freedom makes me powerful. Also, my husband, my family, JiaYi, the women we employ and serve—they make me so much more powerful than I could ever be on my own.

JIAYI: My grandmother has always been a very good example for me of what powerful looks like. She has always encouraged me to pursue my dreams and told me not to be afraid of doing the right thing even when others may disagree. The fact that I finished high school and went to university is a huge example of this, as our village thought education for women was just a waste of money! Because of my grandmother, even as a young girl I started to be assertive and make my own decisions. The women at Freeleaf also amaze me by their power. They may have low education and they have experienced a lot of hurt, but they always try their best to live a good life and provide for their children. Seeing their potential to live the life they want despite their past is a constant encouragement to me.

WOMEN FIGHTING
THE SYSTEM

WHEN IT COMES TO SEEING MORE WOMEN TAKING UP space, raising their voice, and creating change, it often means dismantling the systems that exist and rebuilding with something more inclusive. I think about the women throughout history who have carried out bold acts, taken incredible risks, and dared to step out of line and out of expectations placed on them, whose actions have echoed throughout generations in a way that makes us marvel that there was a time when we couldn't do things like vote, drive, work outside the home, open our own bank accounts, or buy property.

Everyone is familiar with Nelson Mandela. But none of his activism and the continuation of the antiapartheid movement would've been possible without his former wife Winnie Mandela, who became a prominent and controversial figure in her own right. She led marches, gave public speeches, and was even looked to as the leader in what was considered a very violent faction of the movement, while her husband was in prison. She was elected to parliament later in her life, where she served up until her death in 2016. Despite her polarizing actions, she was nicknamed the Mother of the Nation for her fierce dedication to ending apartheid.

I think of the British suffragettes, as popularized in the 2015 movie *Suffragette,* who risked it all so that women across Britain would have the right to vote. They did not ask politely; they stood up, raised their voices, in some instances were violent, and, tragically, some even died for the cause. Despite the risks, they foresaw the future and knew fighting for the ballot for women was worth it all.

I think of the Saudi Arabian activists who have faced jail and other scary circumstances, all because they chose to defy the Kingdom's ban on women driving. In 2014 Loujain al-Hathloul drove from the United Arab Emirates into Saudi Arabia while filming herself, and released the video publicly. She was then arrested and sent to jail. A number of other activists have joined her in this fight, which has been gaining attention from women's groups and feminists across the world, but sadly many of them have been put in jail and are still there today. In 2018, however, the ban on women driving had been lifted, and in 2019 the travel ban was lifted. While a number of activists remain in jail, we know that without them daring to step out of line, progress would not have been possible.

Change does not always come comfortably, but nothing worth fighting for is ever easy. It often involves risk, as the women in this chapter will share. What these women have taught me is that you can be loud, but you can also be quiet and move mountains as well as change hearts and minds. What we've been told to think of as "strength" comes from a typically masculine definition—physical abilities, authoritative, loud, brash, abrasive, etc. But being strong also means being emotionally vulnerable, being loyal, being consistent, and having the ability to speak to those on the margins of society who are often ignored.

SAGE PAUL

REMEMBER THE NAME SAGE PAUL. SHE IS GOING PLACES.
The work she is doing within the fashion community in Canada,
specifically for Native designers and artists, is making the fashion
world take notice. With numerous awards and design accolades, Sage
is at the top of her game.

Sage is the founding collective member and artistic director of
Indigenous Fashion Week Toronto, which is all about amplifying
the work and artistry of Indigenous designers and artisans. They
aim to prioritize Indigenous designers (at least 60 percent) and
have a majority Indigenous female creative team working behind
the scenes.

The mission of IFWTO is to disrupt mainstream cultures while
also educating people about the harm of exploiting Indigenous
textiles, narratives, and stereotypes. This type of message is also
something Sage brings into the academic arena with her role as
board advisory at the Ryerson School of Fashion, and to George
Brown College, where she is developing an Indigenous Fashion
elective course.

Sage's work, which she calls "antifashion," is about showing the
deep connections to people, culture, the land, and most importantly
the Indigenous way of life. I spoke with this cultural and artistic
disrupter about IFWTO, her heritage, and how fashion can become
a powerful vehicle to share vital cultural messages.

When did you first become interested in fashion and design as you were growing up?

Fashion was instilled in me at a young age. My family and community made our own fashion, regalia, and crafts, because it's culturally our way of life. Fashion, crafts, and textiles are forms of Indigenous expression, culture, and storytelling that only we can share. For example, right now I'm really into exploring the Witiko spirit [an Indigenous evil or cannibalistic spirit], and the correlations between cannibalism and capitalism—and that moves me in profound ways to ensure we are a part of and have access to the larger Canadian dialogue, where we create and disseminate our own work.

Tell me about your Indigenous background.

I am proud to be Denesuline Tskwe and a member of English River First Nation. My family and ancestors fought and continue to fight through oppression and colonialism so I could be here. Because of that, I feel like the work I do is bigger than I am. I hold a responsibility to those after me. That is what being an urban Denesuline woman is about.

On your website, you have the words "anti-fashion" on the homepage. Can you tell me what this means?

"Mainstream fashion" is a commodity that functions in capitalism. With the focus on profits mainstream fashion exploits the consumer for sales. Marketing and advertising illusions are released to increase sales. They use alluring images and words like "fashionista," "must-have," and "luxury." Antifashion is conscious and resists that illusion. For me, antifashion is to make and share fashion as a form of expression, a language, and a tool. Fashion can unify and connect people, culture, history, politics, religion, trends, scenes, and more. Fashion is a powerful inclusive medium and can be the precursor to something meaningful if approached with strategy, care, and integrity.

You are the founder of Indigenous Fashion Week Toronto, an event that celebrates and showcases the work of majority Indigenous designers and textile creators. Why did you create this event?

It was time. We need and deserve our own platform to present our work. Every person undeniably interacts with fashion every single day and Indigenous designers play an important role in that interaction. Right now there is a very visible movement of Indigenous fashion, crafts, and textiles, and because of that I'm excited for the perspective of fashion to go beyond commerce and towards culture and arts. IFWTO presents 100 percent Indigenous designers and artists in fashion, crafts, and textiles; the majority are women.

> I HOLD A RESPONSIBILITY TO THOSE AFTER ME. THAT IS WHAT BEING AN URBAN DENESULINE WOMAN IS ABOUT.

Given that the fashion industry has historically been notorious for exploiting and excluding Indigenous designers and stories, what does it mean to you to be able to disrupt this world while also using it as a platform for the Native voices?

Only ten years ago the opportunity for Indigenous designers to be included in the fashion industry beyond a token was incredibly difficult. Our trailblazers and leaders a decade ago, and decades before that, have empowered someone like me to carry that legacy of work.

We are at an incredible place right now—not just in fashion, but also in music, film, TV, literature, and performance. We are being invited into mainstream spaces and, more importantly, we are creating our own spaces. There's a movement of Indigenous arts happening around the world.

But, there will always be more work to be done.

Your own collection, Giving Life, debuted at the Fashion & Design Festival in Montreal at the end of August, and each piece told parts of your personal story of trauma and treatment within the hospital system. Can you share more about this?

I've experienced malpractice in the health system three times where my life was at risk. I can't say whether or not this was because I'm an Indigenous woman, because I'm a woman, or because I was young, but I do know I was not provided the care I needed until a very critical, scary moment. It's scary to not trust a system that is meant to provide health care. My collection "Giving Life" is a protest or cleanse of failed systems.

What makes you a powerful woman?

I have issues with how power is misused and I steer from words that can be misconstrued to disempower others. To label someone as a powerful person can become fraught. There are so many traits and values I see in my leaders and role models that I try to reflect in my day-to-day. Some of the most important are active listening, generosity, and curiosity.

ANGELINA ASPUAC

BY ELIZABETH ROSE

ANGELINA ASPUAC IS A FORTY-YEAR-OLD MAYAN woman living in Sacatepéquez, Guatemala. She is a daughter of farmers, a mother of three children, a wife, and a third-year law student. She is also a spokesperson for the Women's Development Organization of Sacatepéquez (AFEDES), and defended a bill before the Guatemalan courts in 2016. The bill asked that the Guatemalan copyright laws protect the Maya community from copyright infringement of their traditional designs by national and multinational companies. This would give the community of Mayan weavers sole authorship over their artistic designs and the same protections now afforded musicians and authors.

The copying of designs is common in the fashion industry. In February 2017 the Maasai of Tanzania and Kenya created the Maasai Intellectual Property Initiative (MIPI) to protect their iconic designs. They have estimated that eighty companies are now infringing to the tune of ten million dollars per year.

The Maya hope to stop infringement of their designs by hundreds of companies and small entrepreneurs inside and outside of Guatemala. The use of textiles made by poor women has become an industry for national and international companies placing the materials on high-end products such as purses, belts, and shoes. None of these products return income to the artisans who make the textiles. The Maya consider it theft and cultural appropriation to steal their work and copy their designs. They receive neither compensation nor recognition.

Angelina spoke about how the Maya are also exploited by the government bureau of tourism (INGUAT), which uses the indigenous culture as a tourist attraction but doesn't compensate the community for the income that flows from international travel. The Maya are seen as a "folklorized" culture and not recognized as authentic Guatemalan culture.

This is a struggle that is largely a poor woman's struggle and comes twenty-two years after the Peace Accords of 1996 ended the Civil War that took two hundred thousand lives, 83 percent of them Mayan. It is the women weavers who are staging a fight for their equal rights and recognition of their place in society.

You are part of a grassroots women's organization that is fighting to protect ancestral traditions and customs of the Maya. Could you tell us what is the relevance for your community?

The importance of the work we do, specifically the defense, protection, and custody of our weavings and ancestral knowledge, is intimately linked to our identity and the care of life. There's a lot of knowledge and ancestral wisdom that is still available, but it is being lost and devalued due to globalization, where everything is viewed through the lens of monetary value, and not in the value of life. The work we do is closely tied with recuperating all the knowledge linked to our identity and then the recovery of the hands-on work in the weaving.

How is this especially a woman's struggle?

Our organization is made of primarily Maya women. Our struggle has been going on since 1980. This organization came about because there is a big problem with malnutrition, violence against women, and illiteracy.

The weavings are a part of what we do in terms of the care of life and the autonomy of our people. The care of life is not just taking care of our families or our communities, it is everything.

We are demanding that a law be established that will protect our weavings as part of that thread of the care of life. It would be ideal if things could be commercialized and there were benefits for the community. Given that so much is exported by companies abroad, we hope that they too can give back to the communities so that we will not lose the art of weaving and sustaining life in our communities.

This is where AFEDES tries to help women to contextualize their situations, and not to simply accept what comes our way, but to see things more critically and express and demand our rights.

You have called the use of indigenous designs "plagiarism." Why?

When fashion companies advertise their products and assemble Maya pieces, or from other indigenous people, they claim to be inspired by Mayan culture. For a long time we accepted all the talk of inspiration; we even read on the Internet how good it is that our culture is being made known to the world. But once it is viewed through an economic point of view, it is truly an unscrupulous way to take advantage of indigenous people, given that *they* are making a profit through these creations and designs, not the indigenous people.

Nor are the companies looking to see how they can give back to our communities. When we look at the numbers, and see how much they pay indigenous people for the work, and how much they sell it for, it is evident that we get next to nothing. When this happens, it cannot be said that indigenous people are an inspiration; rather, what is happening is theft. We are not prohibiting the commercialization, we are not against our textiles being used and sold, but if they are to be sold and profits are to be made, let it be done with clear rules.

How can consumers stop buying designs that should be protected?

When you enter a store and choose what to buy, there should be some information on the label indicating what town or people made the item, who the authors are, and whether they are paying author rights or usage rights for the reproduction of their design. I think consumers could demand that type of information.

WE ARE NOT AGAINST OUR TEXTILES BEING USED AND SOLD, BUT IF THEY ARE TO BE SOLD AND PROFITS ARE TO BE MADE, LET IT BE DONE WITH CLEAR RULES.

What would you say is the importance of AFEDES in fighting to preserve and protect the Indigenous culture for future generations of women?

Indigenous women are not seen as attorneys, architects, and engineers, but rather like servants, especially when we wear our attire in the capital, at the university, in schools, and in institutes. There are ideas and stereotypes regarding being indigenous as different and that is not favorable. It is also economics, which is closely linked to racism, that does not allow us to act freely and demonstrate our identity to the world, where we come from, and what our roots are. We are not taught in school about the richness of Maya culture. One starts to deny one's identity, until we reach spaces like AFEDES and other organizations that are working towards strengthening our identity. When we learn about all that the Maya civilization has contributed to humanity we feel very proud. I think that it is important to recognize the contributions that civil associations in Guatemala are making to strengthen this identity.

[Elizabeth Rose is a North American writer and journalist. She prefers to write about the environment and social justice. She is currently at work on a memoir about her work with the Guatemalan nonprofit Long Way Home over the past thirteen years. While visiting Guatemala she made many friends, and she hopes to bring their stories to a wider audience. She has previously published articles and essays in Truthout, Ms. *magazine online,* The Boston Globe Magazine, The Worcester Journal, *and* Revue *magazine. She lives in Massachusetts with her husband. Her website is elizabethannerose.com.]*

NDUMIE FUNDA

BY HANNAH MEYER

IN 2008, NDUMIE FUNDA FOUND HERSELF GRAPPLING with the deaths of her fiancée, Nosizwe Nomsa Bizana, and close friend, Luleka Makiwane. Both women had died of AIDS contracted during violent "corrective" rapes. No one paid much attention.

Corrective rape is a hate crime, where men rape women thought or known to be gay, ostensibly to "cure" them of their homosexuality. Though up to ten gay women are raped each week in Cape Town alone, in 2008 it was still an obscure issue, part of the long-ignored epidemic of violence that terrorizes South Africa's LGBT community.

Being ignored, however, was not part of Ndumie's constitution. Given that she was a product of South Africa's student resistance, the only response she ever considered was to fight for justice. Ndumie founded a grassroots NGO named Luleki Sizwe, to support victims of corrective rape, and commenced what is now a nearly decade-long campaign of intensive and outspoken activism against the violent oppression of South Africa's LGBT community.

Ndumie does not want to dwell on the horror of the crimes she has worked so hard to end. Instead, she chooses to share how one woman has succeeded in gaining so much for the LGBT community in South Africa and her thoughts on where today's young activists are going astray in their efforts to bring about positive change.

She believes it is important for the world to understand about other countries and the work they are doing.

"You cannot just turn a blind eye, our work needs to be acknowledged," she said.

Forcing people to see and acknowledge is something of Ndumie's specialty. Her activism is unrelenting and has transformed the once marginalized issue of corrective rape into a symbol of the violent persecution of South Africa's LGBT community. The result has been a series of extraordinary triumphs for LGBT rights.

Since founding Luleki Sizwe, Ndumie has led a Change.org petition that earned 170,000 signatures and pushed the South African government to recognize corrective rape as a hate crime. She has fought for and participated in a new government task force on gender-based violence. And she has secured the participation of South Africa's religious leaders in addressing violence against the LGBT community.

SO, YES, MY LIFE IS IN DANGER, BUT THIS IS MY CALLING AND I WILL LIVE MY STRUGGLE IN THE TOWNSHIPS.

"It simply means that persistence and perseverance does work if you know your story and you are dedicated and committed to continue doing the work that you do," she said.

Though Ndumie has grown accustomed to working alongside the upper echelons of South Africa's leadership, she has remained loyal to her people on the ground. She works in the townships with Luleki Sizwe to rescue and support victims of corrective rape and uses her own home as a safe house, an act of generosity that has put her life in considerable danger.

"I have sold my house, moved to another area I don't know how many times just trying to get to a place of safety. So, yes, my life is in danger, but this is my calling and I will live my struggle in the townships," she said.

It is, however, the survival of grassroots organizations like Luleki Sizwe that causes Ndumie the most concern, as they don't always get the recognition or support they need to continue the work.

"You cannot sideline [grassroots organizations]. Those are the people who know every corner of this country where I live, the townships, and the lifestyle of the people in those black communities."

But this appears to be exactly what has happened. While Ndumie's work with the South African government has seen her awarded France's Ordre National du Merite, her grassroots efforts with Luleki Sizwe still struggle to obtain adequate support. Likewise, for all the recent attention paid to protecting LGBT rights in South's Africa's legislation, young black gay men and women in the townships continue to suffer increasingly violent forms of discrimination.

"Young gay men and women are being mistreated at school and the first people that are doing that are the teachers. They end up being dropouts, exposed to drugs, they are raped while at school, and so forth," she said.

While Ndumie has successfully engaged young voices within her own community to campaign against the treatment of gay men and women in South Africa's schools, she wonders about the state of activism among the youth further afield.

"I have traveled overseas and I have been granted opportunities of addressing different audiences. In the United States the younger generation nowadays are very vibrant, but they lack the knowledge of understanding who they are. There is energy there, but they need to be trained, they need to understand all the issues that affect society at large," she said.

Ndumie points especially to the limits of online activism. She warns that while young people are connecting with issues overseas in ways that were previously not possible, they are lacking important connections with those who are "hands-on" with issues on the ground.

"I tend to differ with other people and their way of thinking. It is not about having five thousand people in your database and saying you are making an impact. The very same people who are working with the database are making no impact."

Ndumie does not hesitate to offer us the guidance we need to start making real change: get back to grassroots activism, stay committed, and connect with as many other organizations as you can, working at all levels—from the ground up to the highest rungs of parliament. Effective and smart activism puts pressure on as many points as possible.

"Who are we changing? I am not changing my own gay people. Transformation should be made in people who are having a problem with gender issues: the perpetrators, the community, the government," she insists.

But the most insistent of all Ndumie's advice is to take action on the issues that matter, just because it is a vital "part of being a principled person." And perhaps, there should be no motivation more compelling than that.

[Hannah Meyer recently graduated with an MA in human rights and now intends to engage her pen with her passion for feminism. She lives out of a backpack and has traveled around the globe, including stretches working with refugee communities in Thailand and India.]

SHIRA TARANTINO

BY AMBER FRENCH

WE'RE ALL AWARE OF THE GUN VIOLENCE EPIDEMIC that has plagued America for many years now. While most of America seems to be on the same page about common-sense gun laws, the politicians, whose pockets are deep with NRA money, pose a roadblock for those trying to implement change that is so desperately needed. We've seen a shift like no other, thanks to the force and drive of the Parkland students in Florida.

We've also seen collaboration and passion born out of grassroots groups that all typically begin from the idea of one person and that then go on to do many impactful things. These are the unsung heroes of our country. The ones giving birth to the ideas that will cause real change, organizing on the ground, staying up all hours of the night planning vigils, rallies, and organizing the people who all have the same end goal.

One of those unsung heroes, Shira Tarantino, is a real-life Wonder Woman living in Stamford, Connecticut, with her husband and two children, who rallies, fights, organizes, and blazes trails with contagious passion. Shira started the Stamford Pediatric Gun Safety Project, is on the Board of Directors for Connecticut Against Gun Violence (CAGV), and is a member and lead organizer of The ENOUGH Campaign.

The horrific day of the Sandy Hook shooting in Newtown, Connecticut, was the impetus for Shira's involvement in each of these

Michael Hyman, US Senator Richard Blumenthal,
Mayor David Martin, Shira Tarantino (left to right)

organizations. The ENOUGH Campaign was organized by Medha Thomas, a mom who, much like many other parents, was deeply impacted by this tragedy. In the very early stages, The ENOUGH Campaign was approached by national organizations like Moms Demand Action and Moms Rising to become a local satellite. Shira says they declined because The ENOUGH Campaign felt that they'd be able to have more control over their work as an autonomous organization.

"The ENOUGH Campaign, CT Against Gun Violence, and other local civic action groups are able to create and collaborate on events and projects which move gun safety forward on a local level. But I am still grateful to Moms Demand, who are dedicated to gun safety vital to the cause," she said.

Shira later started the Stamford Pediatric Gun Safety Project. This was the result of her being a student of the Stamford PLTI (Parent Leadership Training Institute), which is a program of the local nonprofit SPEF (Stamford Parent Education Foundation). The PLTI is a twenty-week family civics course to "improve the lifelong health, safety, and learning of Connecticut's children by helping parents and others who care about children develop the leadership skills to make real change—in schools, communities and state and local government."

PLTI students must create a community project, and the Stamford Pediatric Gun Safety Project was Shira's.

"PLTI graduates have gone on to serve in public offices. They establish programs, nonprofit organizations, and scholarships and lead community initiatives, and work in many ways to improve the lives of Stamford children, families, and residents. The PLTI was in its eighteenth year when I became a student in 2017," said Shira.

Her first class was held on January 21, 2017, the same day as the now-historic Women's March.

"Before I had been accepted as a student, I had been planning on being a bus captain to take women from Stamford down to Washington, DC, but decided I had to cancel if I wanted to be a part of the PLTI. There was a local march as well, and we could see a sea of pink hats headed towards Mill River Park from our class window in the Government Center. While I was sorry to miss the march, I knew I had made the right decision."

Shira recently joined the Board of Directors of CT Against Gun Violence.

"The organization, now in its twenty-fifth year, is revisiting its strategic plan, and I am excited to be a part of it. Legislatively, Connecticut should strengthen our firearm storage safety laws, and that's something which I'm fully behind and willing to work on, which would certainly support this project's mission," she said.

The latest gun violence prevention initiative Shira has been working on is SPEAK YOUR TRUTH: Student Open Mic Night.

"This event was born out of the March For Our Lives Stamford rally last spring, where an amazing array of local students responded thoughtfully to the Marjory Stoneman Douglas High School shooting in Parkland, Florida, where seventeen students and educators were shot and killed. Attended by three thousand

> I COULDN'T BE PASSIVE. I THOUGHT, HOW CAN I CONTINUE TO SUPPORT LOVE IN A WAY THAT MAKES A DIFFERENCE AND PREVENTS TRAGEDY? I PERFORM WEDDINGS; LOVE IS MY DRIVING FORCE.

community members, the rally became a cathartic platform for our local students to express themselves politically and socially, instantly defining a need for youth expression and activism. I worked on Speak Your Truth with the same leaders as March For Our Lives in Stamford," she said.

"Speak Your Truth became especially important to us since we received the devastating news of the Stamford student, Marcus Hall, who was shot and killed here in Stamford just a few weeks ago. I feel that events like Speak Your Truth support healthy teen development and strengthen peaceful communities. I participated in the rally and vigil for Marcus Hall. The event was created by Wil Joseph, the founder of Hoops4All, who had lost his brother Max to gun violence last year."

Shira collaborated on the past two Wear Orange events, and spoke at and fundraised for the Disarm Hate rally in Washington, DC, following the Pulse Nightclub shooting in 2016. In addition to all the good Shira is doing for the world, she also works for a magazine she created more than a decade ago called *Handfastings Magazine*.

"*Handfastings Magazine* offers access to and inspirations for Nature-based wedding rituals to brides and grooms who do not have a specific religious affiliation, who are interfaith, or who are Pagan in their spirituality. I am ordained and can perform weddings in NYC, NY State, and Connecticut. But I refocused my creative energies into gun violence prevention following the Sandy Hook massacre. I couldn't be passive. I thought, how can I continue to support love in a way that makes a difference and prevents tragedy? I perform weddings; love is my driving force."

[Amber French resides in New England and is a working mom of two rambunctious boys. She enjoys kitchen dance parties, blogging about life, and home DIY projects. She hopes that through her stories you will see that your life is what you choose to make it—no matter what kind of good, bad, or ugly you've been through.]

ARISSA HALL

MOST PEOPLE ARE FAMILIAR WITH THE STATISTIC THAT the United States is home to the world's largest incarcerated population. It is also important to recognize how, right now, the rates of incarcerated women are growing faster than those of men. Many of the women in prison today are there simply because they cannot afford bail while their trial awaits. This means their families, and especially younger children, are disproportionately impacted by a punitive system that does not take into account the burden it places on people without access to finances to keep them out of prison. It should also be no secret that black and brown women make up the majority of those imprisoned because they can't afford bail.

One organization that has recognized this impact and is working to change the outcomes for a number of women is the National Bail Out collective, which has been spearheading a really important campaign called #FreeBlackMamas, which started in 2017. NBO's Black Mamas Bail Out initiative raises money, which is then posted as bond for black mamas in prison, and it means they can stay and look after their families in the meantime. NBO Project Director Arissa Hall has been leading this initiative across the US and has seen some major media and social attention being raised about the underlying issues, as well as the work her organization is doing. According to her, there are roughly seven hundred thousand people in prison right

now who haven't been convicted of a crime, but are there simply because they can't afford bail.

The Prison Policy estimates that nearly 70 percent of women who are in jail because they can't afford bail are mothers of children under sixteen. The cash-bail system is not an isolated issue; it affects so many aspects of a mother's life, and there is so much reform work to be done.

Arissa is working to fight a system that is doing more damage than good. Being a mother herself, she recognizes the importance of grassroots activism, community involvement, and ensuring that financial status isn't the determining factor of your freedom.

How did you first get involved with the National Bail Out organization, and can you tell us about your role there today?

I got involved with what would become the National Bail Out collective prior to its formation, back in January 2017, while attending a bail meeting for black organizers that was convened by Color of Change and Movement for Black Lives. It was during that meeting that Mary Hooks, the codirector of Southerners on New Ground, shared the idea of doing a bail-out, which became a collective commitment called Black Mamas Bail Out. At the time, I was working with bail funds across the country to assist in their formation and general technical assistance, so I was elected the leader to help build the infrastructure to actualize that commitment—which would become National Bail Out.

There is such a wide variety of people involved running NBO, from professionals to those with proximity to the prison system. Why do you feel this diversity is important to your work?

It represents all of the talents and wisdom that we need to win and do this work well. We believe that those who are experts and fit to lead are those that are closest to the problems, and thus closer to the ability to mold the solutions. We want to disrupt the idea that only a holder of certain professional experiences and degrees, without any lived or communal experience, was better equipped to lead, as it has often led to harmful reforms made in our name, but without our involvement.

There has been a lot of mainstream media attention about the #FreeBlackMamas campaign. How did this idea come about?

#FreeBlackMamas is a national campaign and rallying cry to free black mothers and caregivers from jails and immigrant detention centers by posting their bail for Mother's Day, with the Black Mamas Bail Out. The Black Mamas Bail Out was conceptualized during the aforementioned meeting of black organizers in 2017, who came together to strategize about interventions to the money bail system that predominantly entraps black communities, with a guiding question of "what can we do together that we cannot do by ourselves?" Mary Hooks shared the idea of doing a bail-out and Black Mamas Bail Out and the #FreeBlackMamas campaign were born. It received so much attention because we were clear in our mission and ask, while doing this around a beloved holiday for the people in our communities. Many folks shared with me that they donated to #FreeBlackMamas in their mother's name or with their mother, and that was powerful.

Can you share some of the ways National Bail Out helps mothers regain life skills and other modes of confidence after they are bailed out?

I want to note that we don't only bail out cis women, but also trans women and femmes, as we recognize the ways that these systems harm and further marginalize these identities, which is why we say "mamas and caregivers." We have a robust supportive services infrastructure that we had to create following the first bail-out as we realized that some of our people have immense needs. We began by providing support that ranged from transportation to and from court to case management and drug rehabilitation. In addition, we were clear that we wanted the mamas to join the journey while also being able to be supported and developed as leaders in intentional ways. So we launched the Free Black Mamas fellowship under the visionary leadership of Je Naè Taylor, of member group Gilda Papoose Collective, which was an eight-week political education fellowship that culminated at an in-person conference hosted by The National Council of Incarcerated and Formerly Incarcerated Women and Girls, where they were able to meet and build community.

What are some of the reasons for women being the fastest-growing population in US prisons today?

The reasons for this are diverse but ultimately a reflection of the patriarchal society in which we live and how it treats and underserves those that are not cisgender men. We know that a vast majority of women in prisons are sexual and physical abuse survivors and more likely to suffer from mental illness, which becomes exacerbated in prison. This can lead to further criminalization that worsens their sentences. There is also no prison reform to address the female prison population and their specific criminalization. The recent reforms that have reduced the prison population for men have not done the same for women. Most women in prison are mothers, which has a significant impact on the children, as they are usually the primary caretakers, which in turn causes family separation. This can destabilize a family and community rapidly.

WE BELIEVE THAT THOSE WHO ARE EXPERTS AND FIT TO LEAD ARE THOSE THAT ARE CLOSEST TO THE PROBLEMS, AND THUS CLOSER TO THE ABILITY TO MOLD THE SOLUTIONS.

Would you say grassroots activism and community is the secret to the organization's success?

Definitely. NBO was able to be successful due to people believing enough in our work to donate and support the vision. During our first Black Mamas Bail Out we raised seven hundred thousand dollars from thousands of people who believed in our ability to free our people and understood the urgency of the work. It is due to them and others who also said "yes" to our commitment to #FreeBlackMamas that we can do the transformational and innovative work that has seen the release of over 430 individuals so far.

You are working to empower and give power back to so many lives, especially black mamas. But I'd like to know what makes YOU a powerful woman.

I'm a powerful woman because I'm a woman and black mama that is willing to do what it takes to achieve collective liberation and be transformed in its service. I was also pregnant when cocreating National Bail Out and Black Mamas Bail Out, which somehow makes me miraculous in addition to powerful!

FRAIDY REISS

PEOPLE OFTEN REFER TO THE UNITED STATES AS "the most powerful nation on earth," but I find myself questioning who has power in this country, specifically. Because when you start to zoom in on certain issues, you realize there are many issues that render individuals powerless, where activism is needed more than ever. Child and forced marriage is one of those issues. Yes, I'm talking about child and forced marriage in the United States. In case you were wondering, until 2018, child marriage was legal in all fifty states. That year, thanks to the tireless activism of a nonprofit organization called Unchained at Last, together with legislators, two states passed laws explicitly banning the practice—Delaware and New Jersey. A quarter of a million American children were married by consent of their parents, a judge, or both between 2000 and 2010. Unchained at Last was started by Fraidy Reiss, who herself is a forced marriage survivor. In her widely shared TEDx Talk where she talks about this awful practice, she candidly talks about her own forced marriage at nineteen in a tight-knit religious community, and having to eventually escape a violent and abusive situation with her daughters in tow. The work she is doing today is nothing short of heroic. Through Fraidy Reiss I have learned that real superpowers come from those doing the hard work required to make true and lasting change.

When we think of child marriage we often think of countries across the world, but this is happening in the United States today. Can you give me an overview of the problem?

Most people, I think, have no idea. Whoever we speak to seems to be shocked by this. Our goal here at Unchained at Last is to fight not only child marriage, but also the bigger picture of forced marriage, which can happen to somebody of any age. We do a lot on child marriage because A, it's easy to define, quantify, and legislate; and B, it's easy for people to understand why it's a problem. The bigger picture of forced marriage is a little more complex because no real research has been done in the United States about how often forced marriage is happening. For a long time nobody even knew how often child marriage was happening and we at Unchained at Last changed that. Our groundbreaking research found that between 2000 and 2010 an estimated 248,000 children were married in the United States. They were as young as twelve, possibly even younger. When we did this research in 2015, in more than half of the United States there was no minimum age specified for marriage. And then the other really upsetting data point that we discovered was that almost all of those 248,000 children that were married in that one decade were girls married to adult men.

Why did you start your organization Unchained at Last?

I founded Unchained at Last as a way to help others in the United States who are escaping forced marriages, and it felt really great to be able to take my own trauma and turn it into a way to help others. And then more and more girls under the age of eighteen started reaching out to Unchained to ask for help. This is when I realized that this is not only a huge problem because of the fact that it's legal, but what was so horrific was that there was almost nothing we can do to help a girl who is not yet eighteen to either say "no" to a marriage that's being planned for her, or to escape one that she's already in. Because of the ways the laws are written in most of the

United States, there's almost no recourse for a minor girl that is being forced to marry, or has already been married.

If you are eighteen or older and you call us at Unchained, the first thing we help you to do is leave home and get to a domestic violence shelter. If you're not yet eighteen, in most of the United States, you're considered a runaway. Also, if we help you to leave home before you're eighteen, we could be charged. That actually happened in one of the cases that we worked on. One of our volunteers was charged criminally for helping a fourteen-year-old girl escape. If these underage girls manage to get to a domestic violence shelter on their own, the shelters won't take them in under the age of eighteen because there are all kinds of liability issues and often funding guidelines that prevent them from taking in a child.

Also, you're typically not allowed to bring any legal action in your own name before the age of eighteen. It's usually a parent or a judge or both who enter you into the marriage, and you're completely voiceless throughout that process if you're not eighteen, and you don't even have the legal right to end that marriage. So marriage before the age of eighteen is a trap.

What are some of the most common reasons for child and forced marriage happening in the United States?

There are many reasons. Tradition, whether that's cultural or religious, is a big one, especially with the forced marriage of adults. That was certainly the case in my family.

The girl who is most vulnerable and at the highest risk for forced child marriage in the United States is a pregnant girl. Parents think it is shameful or they think the girl is better off if she gets married. Extensive research in the United States shows the opposite. In some cases a teen girl gets pregnant and parents want to cover up a rape. They don't want a "nice guy" going to prison so the way to make it OK is with a marriage. Often it's someone who is sixteen or seventeen.

IT'S A PRETTY SOMBER EXPERIENCE BUT AN EXTRAORDINARY FEELING, STANDING THERE KNOWING YOU ARE MOVING THE NEEDLE EVER SO SLIGHTLY IN THE DIRECTION OF GENDER EQUALITY.

How do victims find out about Unchained?

Most of them hear about us either through word of mouth, through a Google search, or referrals from law enforcement, the State Department, or domestic violence agencies. The first service that we provide when people reach out is coordinating and implementing escape plans—helping someone leave home and get somewhere safe, like a domestic violence shelter. We also provide free legal representation, whether it's divorce or domestic violence or any other legal needs that survivors have. We don't charge for any of our services; that's all done through our volunteers. Often the legal needs they have are immigration. Sometimes a person is brought from overseas for a forced marriage and doesn't have legal immigration status. Also, it could be a legal name change. There are women who have to change their name legally from a family that refuses to allow them to leave and will continue to search for them and retaliate against them for daring to say no.

Beyond that, it's also rebuilding your life and becoming financially and emotionally independent. We provide all kinds of social services and emotional support to help mostly women and girls achieve that kind of independence. It's everything from English as a second language class to driver's education or help getting into college.

Tell me about your Chain-in events and what happens at them.

A chain-in is a form of protest that we invented here, where we gather usually between thirty and fifty people. We all wear bridal gowns and veils, and we chain our wrists and tape our mouths, and this is a really powerful way to show legislators and the world this is what life looks like for a woman or a girl who is forced to marry. It's a pretty somber experience but an extraordinary feeling, standing there knowing you are moving the needle ever so slightly in the direction of gender equality.

It's hard to ignore a group of chained brides! Apparently legislators find it easy to discount the heartbreaking testimony of the survivors of child marriage who share their story. But what you can't ignore is, on your way to the office, a group of chained brides standing there chanting, "Let's end child marriage!" And because it often gets a lot of media attention as well, it means not only the legislators passing by the actual protest have that double-take, but also everyone who sees it on TV, hears about it on the radio, reads about it in the newspaper, and sees it on social media.

Is there one particular survivor story that stands out to you?

One of the stories that I do have permission to share is actually about our first client. We've got a video of her on our website. She had a very similar story to my own. She was nineteen when she was forced to marry. It was a really abusive, terrible marriage. She had two kids and finally got the guts to leave. The family shunned her for daring to leave, like my family did. We helped her get out of a really terrible situation. She was diagnosed with a really aggressive form of breast cancer, and even though she was sick the family would still not talk to her. I feel very fortunate and privileged to help her through her really difficult journey, to help her get divorced, to get custody of her children, to help her caring for her kids while she was so sick. I was able to babysit them while she had surgery. When she had to go for her treatments she didn't have a car and we were able to get one for her. Unfortunately, a couple of years ago she died. But she was the first person who came to us, and trusted us to support her through that. I'll never forget Jamie.

What are your major goals for the next ten years with Unchained?

Over the next ten years I really hope we can end child marriage in most of the United States, and then start focusing on the bigger picture of forced marriage of adults, which is a much more complicated process.

Finally, what makes you a powerful woman?

I guess it's my relentlessness. There's a power in refusing to give up and refusing to back down. That's what got me through difficult times in my life and helped me get out of some really tough situations. It's also what keeps me going at Unchained at Last. Sometimes I just want to scream and bang my head against the wall, like "Why can't we just agree that a child should not be forced to marry!" How could you not pass common-sense, simple legislation that harms no one and costs nothing, but saves girls' lives? There's a certain relentlessness that's required to be able to hear a legislator say, like I've heard, "What's so bad about a girl marrying her rapist?" A legislator in Nevada actually said that to my face. When you hear these kinds of things again and again, it's the relentlessness that makes me get up the next day and still go back and help people.

WOMEN DISRUPTING
THE STATUS QUO

THE THINGS THAT MAKE US DIFFERENT. . . THOSE ARE OUR SUPERPOWERS.

THAT IS A QUOTE FROM EMMY AWARD–WINNING WRITER and actress Lena Waithe, who stood on the Hollywood stage and paid homage to her cohorts in the LGBTQ community. As an open lesbian, Lena has defied entertainment industry norms and is part of an ongoing cultural conversation dedicated to the need for more diverse representation in media, politics, and society.

In this chapter we are profiling the work of activists, trailblazers, and pioneers, ordinary individuals who show the direct impact diversity and representation has in our communities. Media and entertainment of course plays a large role in enabling us to "see ourselves" in certain ways. Actor Mahershala Ali, the first Muslim to win the Academy Award, in 2017 for Best Supporting Role in *Moonlight*, played a gay, black man struggling to find his identity in a world hostile to the LGBTQ community.

Outside of media, LGBTQ representation is soaring in politics, as we recently saw in the 2018 United States midterm elections. A record number of female and LGBTQ candidates ran for office that year, and more than 240—an unprecedented number—won their primaries. Several of them made history, including the first openly gay man to be elected governor (Jared Polis in Colorado), and a Native American lesbian who won a House seat in Kansas (Sharice Davids), becoming the first queer person to represent the state in Congress.

If we are going to ensure discrimination is completely eliminated, representation and visibility are key.

In this chapter I am celebrating the everyday heroes who are helping break down barriers and fostering self-worth to lift others up who would've otherwise been invisible.

MARIAH HANSON

MARIAH HANSON, FOUNDER OF THE WORLD'S LONGEST-running and largest event for queer women, is badass. The year 2018 marked the twenty-eighth anniversary of The Dinah Shore, a festival Mariah created to be a fun, safe, and supportive environment, which was initially launched to focus on and give voice to the lesbian community. I am in awe of Mariah for daring to be a pioneer at a time when being openly lesbian could have cost her numerous work opportunities. Thankfully she persisted, and today she is inspiring queer women everywhere. Today, The Dinah has become a go-to event for major female pop acts such as Lady Gaga, Katy Perry, Tegan and Sara, Meghan Trainor, Lizzo, Kesha, The Pussycat Dolls, Bebe Rexa, Iggy Azalea, and more. I interviewed Mariah to get her take on female empowerment, our current political culture, and what it means for the LGBTQ community.

The Dinah Shore has been championing female empowerment for decades. Why was this important to you?

My entire career has been dedicated to increasing the visibility of women. Year after year The Dinah continues to affirm its unwavering commitment to focus on the power of women to create big and lasting change. It is important to me to bring female artists to The Dinah who are making it happen for themselves, especially in a male-dominated industry. My goal with this festival is to continue to raise the bar on female achievement with an event that is entirely produced by women, for women.

> WE PURPOSEFULLY SHOWCASE POWERFUL WOMEN AT ALL STAGES OF THEIR CAREER WHO ARE CREATING THEIR OWN SUCCESS AND STAYING TRUE TO THEIR OWN VOICE.

How does The Dinah Shore aim to promote more female-friendly spaces?

For many, The Dinah is an annual destination; for others it is a bucket-list goal, a pilgrimage to our very own queer Mecca. No matter what the impetus for attending is, The Dinah is a unique opportunity to experience one of the most bonding, liberating, and transforming festivals ever in the spirit of sisterhood, womanhood, and community.

We embody the female-friendly space and protect it fiercely. That's not to say men are not welcome at the event. But we hold firmly to the idea that The Dinah is by women, for women, and about women. If men attend, it is as respectful guests.

You experienced your share of naysayers in the beginning. How did you deal with this?

I believe people see life through the eyes of their issues, so if anyone has ever said anything negative about me as a person, I've come to embrace the belief that they are speaking through their own wounds. I have certainly evolved as a human being over the years and am dedicated to making the world a peaceful place to be in. Rather than look toward the naysayers, I choose to simply live every moment at my highest. When I fail, I begin again. The only opinion that truly matters to me at this point in my life is my own.

How does The Dinah Shore fit into the current women's movements we're seeing?

We purposefully showcase powerful women at all stages of their career who are creating their own success and staying true to their own voice. We celebrate women who break glass ceilings day in and day out. We celebrate women who will not be silenced. We offer a platform for empowered female artists to shine as we know that these women are powerful role models. We want our customers to take away the belief that they too can embrace their dreams in their own way on their own terms and in doing so they define their power, and their sovereignty.

SUZANNE SINGER

BY CAMERON AIREN

SUZANNE SINGER IS DOING IMPORTANT WORK IN THE STEM world. She received her PhD in mechanical engineering at UC Berkeley and works as a staff engineer at Native Renewables. In this interview, Suzanne talks about her research in STEM, Native American women in STEM, how society can encourage girls in math, how STEM opportunities for Native Americans can be more accessible, and how feminism can be more inclusive to Native voices.

Tell me about your experience and work as a STEM researcher and developer.

My formal STEM (science, technology, engineering, and math) research experience started when I was an undergraduate student at the University of Arizona. I did well in my thermodynamics class, which led to a one-year research internship. After completing my undergraduate degree, I spent nine months at Intel pushing computer systems to their performance limits to investigate how efficiently heat was managed. During graduate school at UC Berkeley, my research focused on improving power generation by understanding the physics behind heat transfer in materials.

We still see society enforce stereotypes that girls are bad at math. How can we dispose of these stereotypes and encourage and support girls who enjoy/excel in STEM subjects?

Math was my favorite subject in elementary school. I also helped my dad with his engineering endeavors around the house. My parents were both in STEM fields and it was obvious they enjoyed their work. I had teachers that encouraged me to do well in STEM and put me in an accelerated program that did fun science exploration.

I believe that seeing successful people who look like you can break down perceptions of capability and make goals seem more attainable. It's also important to showcase women doing careers that are stereotypically done by men.

What are your thoughts on how STEM can improve to be more inclusive to women, particularly Native women and women of color?

The further I progressed in school, the fewer women of color I saw, particularly in leadership roles. Being one of the few Native American women in the STEM world can feel isolating. In the last few years, I've started hearing the term "unconscious bias," a quick assessment of our situation that we may not be conscious of. This can manifest itself in the workplace and can negatively impact the inclusivity that companies are now aiming to achieve. I would like to see more companies make an effort to educate management and employees about unconscious bias.

Another topic is gender perceptions in the workplace. Numerous articles have been written that highlight the double standard of women's versus men's behavior. I wish women didn't have to worry about being perceived as aggressive in

> I BELIEVE THAT SEEING SUCCESSFUL PEOPLE WHO LOOK LIKE YOU CAN BREAK DOWN PERCEPTIONS OF CAPABILITY AND MAKE GOALS SEEM MORE ATTAINABLE.

professional settings when trying to portray confidence. As a Native person with the cultural respect for elders, one of the hardest things, for me personally, is to be comfortable questioning, disagreeing with, and even teaching or training someone older than myself or in a higher position.

What are some of the socioeconomic barriers that Native Americans face in having access to opportunities in STEM research and education?

Many Native American communities are impoverished and geographically isolated, which leads to educational hurdles. Some homes, including thousands on the Navajo Nation, do not have access to grid-tied electricity. The cost to provide power and heating can be high. Without lighting, it is hard to do homework. Schools might not have access to STEM educational opportunities, resources, or even high-speed Internet access. Without reliable Internet, there are untapped resources for web-based research and education via videoconferencing.

Another barrier is the lack of clear STEM career paths on tribal lands. Very few tribal colleges offer STEM degrees. My perception is that opportunities for STEM (or any) jobs "back home" are very limited. This leads to talented STEM professionals developing and maintaining their expertise elsewhere, when it is greatly needed at home.

Tell me more about your Native American background and how it has influenced and impacts your work in STEM.

I am Navajo (Diné), one of the 566 federally recognized Indian Tribes in the United States. The Navajo Nation is located in Arizona, New Mexico, and Utah, and covers a land base the size of West Virginia. There are over three hundred thousand enrolled members, and over 160,000 live on the Navajo Nation or reservation. The tribe has a rich culture, a language that had a distinguished role in World War II, as well as an evolved three-branch government structure.

I learned at a young age the importance of conserving energy and water because none of my grandparents had these resources easily accessible. I did a lot of reading by dim light for the limited time the kerosene or propane lamps were on. I helped haul water from the local pump in barrels back to my grandparents' house and had to know how to siphon water into buckets, which were then brought in the house. I didn't realize until much later how my experiences on the reservation tied into my current research interests.

How can feminism be more inclusive and uplifting of, and a better listener to, Native voices?

My favorite idea of feminism is equal opportunity for all. I would love for others to understand that many of the struggles that women encounter are also struggles for Native Americans and people of color, both men and women. Having this awareness helps give Native women a voice.

Having the two-way conversation is important. I am personally working on being a better listener. The best discussions are when I try to listen without interrupting and empathize with the other person's point of view. Then they are more willing to listen to my thoughts from a different perspective.

[Cameron Airen is a feminist mind-set coach, gender consultant, mentor and cofounder of the Feminist Coach Academy, Feminist Coach Theory, and the Developing Coach Collective. They help folks of all genders take control of their mind-set, feel more confident, get the life they want, integrate feminism into their work and business, and be gender inclusive. Cam uses they/ she pronouns, is a digital nomad and serves clients all over the globe.]

SHIRA TAYLOR

YOU'D THINK BY NOW, IN THE YEAR 2019, COMPREHENSIVE sex education would be a no-brainer. With numerous studies here in the United States showing that schools implementing fact-based, medically accurate sex education leads to healthier youth, whereas abstinence-only programs lead to higher rates of teen pregnancies and sexually transmitted infections, this shouldn't be such a contentious issue.

Sadly, it still is, not just in the US but in other countries, too, where conservative and religious influences prevent youth from having access to information and education that can help guide them to make positive choices. SExT, or Sex Education by Theatre, founded by Shira Taylor, mixes sex education with performance theater to break down barriers and allow a message to come through in a creative format. SExT has been performed to rave reviews at two of Canada's largest theater festivals, and in front of thousands of high school students, including Indigenous youth in the Northwest Territories. Shira also won a prestigious award for demonstrating excellence in using the arts to address issues of concern in Canada for her work with SExT.

How did the idea for SExT come to fruition?

Fourteen years ago, as a freshman, I sat in the audience at a University-mandated "theatre for social change" spectacle performed by students using pop culture references to tackle topics ranging from "doing

laundry for the first time" to "diversity" to "mental health." Being an eighteen-year-old science major and actress/singer with very limited laundry experience, I remember relating to the scenarios playing out so much that I wanted to jump on-stage myself. As an audience member, and later as a performer and director of this initiative, I remember feeling the energy in the packed hall viscerally shift from one of awkwardness, anxiety, and isolation, to one of relief, joy, and community.

Five years ago, as a doctoral student on a mission, I walked into one of Canada's most diverse and overpopulated high schools, located in an immigration destination of Toronto, with the idea of making sex education more comprehensive, relevant, and impactful by emboldening youth to sing, rap, and dance about everything from chlamydia to homophobia to racism. This visit led me to create the peer education program SExT: Sex Education by Theatre as my PhD thesis, to empower youth from communities where talking about sex is culturally taboo to take center stage. Our main goal is to encourage young people to reflect on, challenge, and communicate their realities and celebrate their unique identities through performance art. Youth are invited to tackle current issues head-on in a nonjudgmental environment that promotes education, discussion, creativity, and personal discovery.

What was your own sex education experience like growing up?

I have one single memory of formal sex education. It involves my grade-nine gym teacher putting a condom on a wooden penis, followed by a heated debate between two girls in the class over whether you could "lose your virginity" via tampon. While I failed to receive any meaningful sex education in school, I did grow up in a very liberal Jewish home where healthy and humorous references to sexuality were often made unfiltered by my parents and grandparents. I also remember my mom would read relevant articles from the daily newspaper aloud from a "knowledge is power" perspective and challenge me to think critically about age-appropriate newsworthy scenarios. I believe my unfiltered access to knowledge growing up can be credited for my being drawn to stigmatized topics professionally. In the case of sex education, I was always fascinated by the concept that so many adults choose to prioritize "protecting" children from sexual knowing on moral, cultural, or religious grounds, despite decades of unequivocal evidence of the devastating physical and mental health consequences of knowledge restriction.

Why do you think there are still a number of countries, even in the developed world, where there is still so much fear-mongering and regressive attitudes toward comprehensive sex ed?

I think it's important to recognize that people are the product of their sociocultural influences and that people on all sides of this debate truly are just trying to protect their children the best way they know how. Comprehensive sex education is about creating a space where people of all belief systems and identities feel safe and respected and can coexist. My doctoral research shows that educational approaches that are comprehensive, nonjudgmental, culturally relevant, engaging, and fun are most effective at creating a climate of acceptance and promoting health and well-being.

Have you received any backlash since starting the organization?

The area where I started SExT is a popular immigration destination of Toronto with a majority South Asian Muslim population. This community has received significant media attention as the hub of protests opposing comprehensive sex education. Despite the conservative reputation in the area, SExT has actually been extraordinarily well received by young people, teachers, and service providers in the community. One of my main goals with SExT is to embrace culture as enriching the sexual health conversation as opposed to as a barrier to discussing these topics. Our show features music, dance, language, and clothing from the diverse countries of origin of cast members, including Pakistan, Bangladesh, China, Jamaica, Ghana, and Ethiopia. By embracing the rich cultures of our cast, we are able to make the show relatable and inclusive to audiences. In terms of parents, we receive mixed responses. Some parents are very supportive.

In one case, a parent who came to the show expressed disapproval about her daughter learning such lessons outside of marriage, yet the daughter later reported that her mother had become much more open in discussing these topics following the performance.

How has theater become a medium through which important messages can be shared?

Youth need to relate to their sex education to take it seriously, which is rarely the case when lessons are delivered by uncomfortable teachers or outdated films. A great deal of what is known about the use of theater in sexual health interventions can be credited to the developing world. The AIDS pandemic in Africa is said to have given rise to a "theater of necessity," with music, drama, and dance used to provide education and support. I chose theater for its unique ability to make sex education personally relevant and to actively engage young people on complex issues, both intellectually and emotionally.

What is the most common myth you hear about sex ed that you help dismantle?

Myth: When kids learn about sex, they are more likely to have sex.

False. The empirical research consistently shows comprehensive sex education that is nonjudgmental, is scientifically accurate, and teaches communication skills makes kids less vulnerable to risky situations, more likely to ask for help, and more likely to form healthy relationships free from abuse and sexual coercion.

As well as schools, you also perform at festivals and work with Indigenous groups in parts of Canada. Why is this an important aspect of SExT?

After being approached by Roxanne Ma, senior manager of National Youth Awareness Programs at the Canadian Foundation for AIDS Research (CANFAR), SExT embarked on our first national tour. We reached over four thousand students in schools and Indigenous reserves in areas of Canada most affected by HIV.

Our time on the reserves was very special. Some were extremely remote and many youth had never before experienced theater and had limited access to sex education.

What most struck me, however, were the commonalities. After cast member Mary Getachew performed her original song, *Tunnel Vision* (now a music video), about leaving an abusive relationship, a girl in grade six approached her and said, "I've struggled too. And I think it's so brave that you put your struggle into art." We hope our show inspires youth in these communities to do just that.

I CHOSE THEATER FOR ITS UNIQUE ABILITY TO MAKE SEX EDUCATION PERSONALLY RELEVANT AND TO ACTIVELY ENGAGE YOUNG PEOPLE ON COMPLEX ISSUES, BOTH INTELLECTUALLY AND EMOTIONALLY.

What do you envision seeing in society if more youth had access to shame-free sex education that was inclusive?

I believe a society with widespread access to inclusive and shame-free sex ed would be a much healthier society, both physically and mentally. We would see less #MeToo scandals, less bullying, less self-harm and suicide, less people in abusive situations.

Finally, what makes you a powerful woman?

I think that I am a powerful woman because I have had the fortune of being surrounded by strong female role models who have built me up and lead by example. I am relentless in going after what I believe in and was, therefore, able to turn a crazy idea in my head (featuring teens rapping about sexually transmitted infections) into a program that I am very proud of and that has real-world impact. I also always try my best to act with open-mindedness, integrity, and compassion, putting other people first.

CHRISTIN ROSE

OVER THE PAST FEW YEARS WE HAVE WITNESSED THE uprising of some pretty incredible female athletes who have defied stereotypical narratives about women in sports—whether it be Serena Williams proving she is one of the best athletes in the world by surpassing tennis legend Steffi Graf's record of twenty-two Grand Slam titles, Ronda Rousey showing the testosterone-fueled mixed martial arts world that she can bring in millions of dollars and viewers into an arena that previously did not allow women to compete (Ultimate Fighting Championship), or the US Women's National Soccer Team winning their fourth World Cup and demanding equal pay for their accomplishments.

This is now the legacy young girls around the United States are growing up watching. With studies showing how beneficial sports participation can be for a young girl's self-esteem and overall health and well-being, the need for visible role models can never be overstated.

One woman creating more visibility for young girls is photographer Christin Rose, who is the creator of "She Plays, We Win." It is a movement, a photo series, and an advocacy project that showcases a range of young female athletes and shares their stories in order to empower a generation of girls who are at a time in their lives when confidence, sisterhood, and encouragement are crucial elements that can help determine their futures.

What sparked the idea for She Plays, We Win?

I started this project in November 2015. At that time I was searching for a way to give back with my photography, to be a voice for something I really cared about. The day I started photographing these girls and asking them questions about why sports matter, I found myself too. This industry is not easy because it's so competitive. I felt like I needed to do something to stand out. I came to a point in my career where I was looking for inspiration, searching for something that got me excited.

I wanted to shoot something I was passionate about. The same type of courage my life requires right now is the exact same stuff I learned on a softball field when I was ten years old. So I started thinking about my life when I was ten. If somebody older than me (especially a cool older girl) told me I was good at something or that I was pretty, I never forgot it because it gave me loads of confidence. That sentiment is exactly what I want to do on a larger level with #sheplayswewin.

THE SAME TYPE OF COURAGE MY LIFE REQUIRES RIGHT NOW IS THE EXACT SAME STUFF I LEARNED ON A SOFTBALL FIELD WHEN I WAS TEN YEARS OLD.

If other little girls can see images and stories of girls their same age that are doing what they want, rocking their own unique style and following their passions—they will be inspired to do the same. There might be a little girl like Charli, the only girl on her ice hockey team who I photographed. Maybe they will see Charli's image in all of her hockey gear and go sign up for ice hockey too. Charli wants any little girl to know that "it is possible and to not get discouraged no matter what anybody says to you."

We seem to be at a moment where people are talking about the need to show more female athletes. Has this impacted your perspective on SPWW?

It definitely contributes to the overall excitement of the project. The direction the media is continually growing is positive. I don't think my project would have the place it does even ten years ago. Girls are demanding more time on the field, and research in recent years has shown us over and over again the many benefits of growing up with a sport.

I'm just trying to have people talk about that, make it a conversation through words and images that inspire and influence perspective. She Plays, We Win is a place to empower each other and, in the process, realize the power of your own story.

Whether it's equal pay, body image, or fighting for equal air time, it seems there are so many obstacles for female athletes. How do you think these issues affect the young girls you photograph?

These issues are ever present for all ages of young girls and women. They're all faced with obstacles because of their gender. That's why we have to teach the youth about confidence, self-respect, and what equality should look like at a very young age. They are the hope of the future as we hopefully work to reduce these issues in society.

Girls today are faced with an unrivaled amount of pressure. My images are meant to combat this a little and increase self-esteem. If we can prepare girls to be confident, free-thinking, independent women (something that I personally believe can come greatly from participating in sports) and fight for what's right for women as our society progresses, then the world will be a better place.

What reactions have you received from girls who see your photographs?

I've shot over fifteen sports so far and really only feel like I've scratched the surface of what's possible. Getting emails from all over the country on how these photos are inspiring girls to do what they want to and not give up—that is my favorite. To inspire girls I don't even know with positive images?! How did I get so lucky! I love the girls. I love their rad little unique personalities and I love telling their stories so more people can experience all this.

What is your ultimate goal for SPWW, and can you explain your intention behind the "we win" part of the title?

"She Plays, We Win" is meant to be a positive and empowering statement about girls playing sports. It literally means, if young girls participate in sports (and are encouraged, celebrated, and challenged at a young age) we all win as a society.

The simple goal is to celebrate girls everywhere in athletics and be an inspiring contribution to the media and how we view girls. Social media has made connecting with each other easier than ever, but it's also made it easier to bully and bombard young women with confusing and impossible images of beauty and "femininity." We are here to show that strength is beautiful. Perseverance is power. And confidence is super cool.

What makes you a powerful woman?

Freedom. It is important to remember that not every woman in this world has the freedom I'm talking about, and sadly, not everyone is allowed that power.

I am fortunate to be free to dream, free to say what I think, to photograph what I believe. If we can continue to work toward equality, more and more people will have this freedom of thought and expression. I have the freedom to influence people with my art. And that to me is the ultimate power.

DESTRI MARTINO

THERE ARE A NUMBER OF EXCUSES FOR STUDIOS NOT hiring more female directors on some major films. Those include "there aren't many of them that exist," "we just don't think they have what it takes," and this gem that totally ignores the inherent presence of sexism: "the opportunities are there, it's the women that don't take them."

A study that looked at the top-grossing films over a period of five years by major studios showed less than 5 percent of them were directed by women. There is only one woman in history to have ever won the Academy Award for Best Director—Kathryn Bigelow in 2009 for *The Hurt Locker*—and only four women in total have ever been nominated.

A recent example of why there is no excuse to be gender biased in Hollywood is *Pitch Perfect 2*. The sequel was directed by actress Elizabeth Banks (who also stars in the film) and in its opening weekend alone made more money than the first movie in its entirety, raking in seventy million dollars.

One woman decided to flip the script and launch a project that would completely eliminate gender disparity in this field in the future. Los Angeles–based director Destri Martino is the creator of The Director List, a growing database of female directors and their resumes.

The one-thousand-plus women featured collectively have credits from film, TV, commercials, and music videos. The site says it is by no means a comprehensive database, but it should already be a go-to destination for studios and production companies.

Tell us about your background as a filmmaker.

I was a film minor at USC, so I started making Super 8 films in college. My first experience working as a production assistant on an indie feature at the age of nineteen solidified my love for production and being on set. When I graduated, I jumped straight into the production world and did that along with assisting a producer and a director for about six years.

Eventually I made a few short films, a web series (*Mixed Blooms*), and about two hundred corporate videos. I left my day job in order to launch The Director List and work on getting my own feature film off the ground.

At what point did you realize as a director/filmmaker that being a woman in this industry comes with some disadvantages?

Probably as soon as I started looking for work after college. A lot of guys from school seemed to team up right away and start making films, creating production companies, or they'd at the very least give each other work. I did get production work on some of their films, but it was hard for me to be taken seriously as a filmmaker, and especially hard to connect with them in the way dudes connect with their fellow dudes.

It was also hard to find other women who wanted to make movies, so it wasn't like I could just pull together my lady team. I'm sure they were out there, but we didn't have Twitter to help us connect with each other.

Also, on bigger productions I tended to be routed to the office jobs—production secretary, office PA—even though I really wanted to be on set. And of course, any time I pitched project ideas to people in the position to produce them, they were seen as feminine and thus unsellable.

How did the idea of The Director List come about?

From a very young age I kept an eye out for female directors. Again, pre-Internet, they were hard to find—they didn't show up much on *Entertainment Tonight* or in the pages of *Premiere* magazine. I really felt a need to see them and see how they directed.

In 2005, I ended up writing my dissertation about women directors and why there weren't more of them. There were very few big articles on the topic of the lack of women directors at that time. Ultimately, I focused my dissertation on one of the very early steps in the hiring process—creating a director list.

With new technology I was able to make my obsession a visual project. I was really motivated to do that after attending the 2012 Cannes Film Festival and seeing several women-directed films listed in the market catalog. There were many more than even I had expected to see, so I wanted to start keeping track of all the women directors I knew of, and those that I continued to discover.

I ended up using Pinterest to keep track of them. And as my women directors board grew and gained more attention I continued to tell people that there were a lot of women directors. As it grew larger and more people started referring to it, it eventually became time to put all those directors into an easy-to-search database—and that's what I have now on thedirectorlist.com.

How did you collect your huge database?

I collected it over many years, most often referring to festival catalogs for names, since fests tend to have more films by women directors than mainstream Hollywood. Any time I saw a name I didn't know, whether in an article, credits, whatever, I'd make a pin. It is still growing. It's now over one thousand women directors and I've received a flood of submissions since the website launched, so there are still a lot more to add.

Have you had any big responses from studios, agents, production companies, etc. since launching?

I've heard from quite a few agents and managers submitting clients and independent producers who have thanked me for the practical resource as they compile their director lists. I've also seen a lot of industry assistants talking about it on social media, so that's really good. They're often the ones starting the lists for their bosses, so it's important they're aware of an easy way to make those lists more diverse.

Why do you think studios are still unwilling to view female directors as capable as men?

Ignorance. Honestly, it makes no sense. The belief system within Hollywood is still so backwards in so many ways. I used to say it's so 1950s, but I think it's really pre–women's suffrage. There are still a lot of people in the position to hire women directors who seem to think that women are these dainty creatures who can't make decisions for themselves, let alone lead a team. Just totally bizarre.

If there are female directors out there who haven't yet been listed on TDL, how would they get featured?

Send me an email at submissions@thedirectorlist.com and I'll send them the form. But they should only submit if they meet the qualifications—they've directed a feature (narrative or doc), an episode of TV, a national commercial, or they have an extensive music video CV. I hate denying people, but the main purpose of the database is to provide qualified directors for film and TV assignments, so I need to make sure the list contains the names of women with the expected experience for those jobs.

For those who don't meet those qualifications, I would still love to hear from them. I have a Twitter list of over 2,200 women directors and/or women-directed projects and I include women at every level on that. So, they should send me their handles if they aren't on there yet. And I share news about all types of projects and women directors on Twitter and Facebook, so all women directors should feel free to send me links to any big news items.

Finally, what makes you a powerful woman?

I believe change is possible and I'm creating ways to make it so.

NILOUFAR NOURBAKHSH

WHEN WE THINK OF MUSICIANS AND COMPOSERS WHO have defined the classical music genre, we think of Beethoven, Mozart, Schubert, Bach, etc. Even in a modern setting, the classical music world is very male-dominated when you look at all the major symphony orchestras around the world. The absence of women, and especially women of color on a larger scale, means the plethora of diverse voices and lived experiences are not being represented as they should be.

One woman is aiming to change that with her music as well as with an organization she founded to disrupt the status quo, and make space for other women of color. Niloufar Nourbakhsh is a composer who grew up in Iran and eventually made her way to the United States to pursue her dream of music. She did not grow up seeing many female musicians as role models, but now she is in a position to change that. She is the founder of the Iranian Female Composers Association (IFCA), which is dedicated to empowering Iranian women in music and in the arts by fostering originality, honoring diversity, and strengthening equality. She has built up the organization and established it as a force for good within the classical music community, alongside her colleagues Anahita Abbasi and Aida Shirazi.

She is a true trailblazer who didn't allow the lack of opportunities to prevent her from pursuing her ultimate dream.

Growing up in Iran, did you have many female role models you could look up to in terms of musicians or artists?

There were many prominent female pianists that were highly influential, like Delbar Hakimova and Farimah Ghavam-Sadri, but no female composer that I knew about. After being determined that I wanted to pursue a path in music, I applied to a few programs in England and the United States. I was lucky to be given a scholarship to attend Goucher College in Baltimore.

Tell us how the Iranian Female Composers Association came about, and what the mission is.

This association really started from the idea of a concert. I had become familiar with the work of several Iranian female composers in the United States that were from my generation, and I thought it would be significant for us to join forces and present our music in one concert, since something like this had never happened before. As I started to think more about it and converse with these wonderful composers, specifically Anahita Abbasi and Aida Shirazi, it became a much bigger concept.

The foundation of IFCA is inclusivity and sharing a space without having to fit to any particular agenda. We want to support Iranian female-identifying composers by commissioning and performing their music, and invite the world to explore the diverse, artistic voices these women are offering. We also hope to empower and support the younger generation in Iran that faces profound cultural and educational roadblocks in discovering their own voice as an artist.

What barriers have you personally faced in the composing world as a woman and as an immigrant?

As an immigrant, the music community could not have been more loving and supportive towards me as it has been in the past three years; however, many opportunities, specifically in the world of opera, are solely given to green card holders and citizens, and that is something to think about. For example, how can a musician on a DACA status apply to any of the calls for scores and competitions that are not competitive international opportunities? Where can they start their careers?

How does the IFCA empower other Iranian female musicians, and what kind of community engagement/outreach does the group do?

During this past year since our launch concert at National Sawdust in April 2018, we were able to commission three Iranian female composers for premieres in Washington, DC, and New York. With each concert, we aim to bring out the Iranian community into these classical concert halls to engage with the emerging composers of Iran as well as becoming involved with the new music scene.

If you could change one thing in the world with music, what would it be?

Music education! Every child deserves to have access to an instrument and a music teacher to explore and express themselves. All children are creative, and it would be a different world if we all grew up without forgetting our playful soul.

Finally, what makes you a powerful woman?

I'm not sure powerful is the exact right word. I think knowing my capacity to love other people and make strong collectives with them gives me joy; but most importantly, understanding my responsibility towards other people, both as a musician and as an individual, gives me a lot of strength.

VELVET D'AMOUR

VELVET D'AMOUR IS A FORCE TO BE RECKONED WITH in the fashion world. As a super plus-size model, she has not only been part of smashing narrow ideals, she is also a photographer and magazine publisher creating opportunities for many other underrepresented people in fashion and beauty.

In 2007 a photo of the American-born, France-based beauty went viral. It was an image of her wearing a red T-shirt stating "please feed the models" as a response to the tragic deaths of two Brazilian models who battled bulimia and anorexia. She left the United States early in her modeling career for the French capital of Paris and found a way forward in a country that, although it still boasts its own problematic beauty ideals, was much more open to new talent and different body shapes and sizes. In 2006 she made international headlines for appearing in John Galliano and Jean Paul Gaultier's shows at a time when plus-size models were still not as visible or accepted as they are today.

A pioneer in her own right, she knew that waiting for someone to give her her "big break" wasn't ultimately what she wanted. She channeled her creative passion of photography and art into *Volup2*—the magazine she launched in 2012 that is today dedicated to editorials and visual stories that show the world fashion is much more than the same old, same old we seem to see in a large majority of magazines.

Velvet isn't content to rest on her laurels and wait for change; she is creating it.

Did you struggle with body image based on the images of women you saw in media and fashion growing up?

I grew up in Rochester, New York. I became fat after a traumatic incident when I was seven years old, and was bullied to the point of having to change schools. My mom's way of dealing with that was to sign me up for swim team. So I was now fat *and* in a swimsuit. I was put on diets growing up to try to curtail the fat that came about after the trauma.

Being bullied definitely led to feeling outcast and I think in an odd way being more "dependent" on my personality than my looks. But cheerleaders were what we were meant to aspire to back in the 1980s, so the fact that I did

swim team, and then was on the track team doing shot put and discus again, meant that my body wasn't conforming to the more popular aesthetic at the time.

Throughout my childhood I was fascinated with images from the 1940s as I would so often peruse my parents' old photos; thus I loved the massive shoulder-padded silhouettes of designers like Thierry Mugler and Claude Montana. I was drawn to the more extreme designers like Mugler and JP Gaultier. I loathed the conservative preppy nature of most American designers like Ralph Lauren and Laura Ashley.

My journey to self-confidence was forged in my twenties when I started to question modern-day beauty ethics based on the fact that I had gained weight through dieting.

How did you get into fashion and photography?

I grew up getting lost in art and when I first began college was a fine art major. Later I had to take a photography course. I was always quite intimidated by technology, but I learned how to master my Pentax K1000 and the rest was history. I spent a year abroad studying in Florence, Italy.

At an underground nightclub I happened to be at, I noticed a beautiful couple—two stunning men with matching mushroom haircuts and protruding collarbones, entirely clad in black. I really wanted to photograph them and when I did ask, they were flattered and I made very beautiful portraits of them, which led me to a series shooting gay guys who were in love. I had lost friends to AIDS and so it meant a lot to me to support the community through my work.

My college internship was for a company that represented fashion photographers and hair and makeup artists and they ended up hiring me out of college.

In 2006 you made international headlines for appearing in shows for John Galliano and Jean Paul Gaultier. How did you feel being part of these shows?

These were the men who helped shape my love of fashion. There were no images in popular media of anything even remotely close to my own appearance, so I could only go to the museum to see one close to my own. That is what made it click that every era has its own icon of modern beauty and that essentially some women will always be feeling left out because their body, shape, color, size, age, etc. isn't what is aspired-to in that time and space. There were no bloggers at the time, so my images were seen as rather in-your-face and controversial. It was how I ended up getting signed to a model agency here in Paris. I was near three hundred pounds and I was thirty-nine years old when I got signed and then I ended up at castings for these shows and my portfolio and personality won them over.

Your foray into mainstream fashion also came at a time when there were serious discussions about unhealthy body representations on catwalks and in magazines. Why did you want to be part of this?

I was in a unique position as a fat female fashion photographer. So many women worshiped supermodels and the powers they held. Many women longed to be a model and saw that as *the* ticket to happiness.

When I was shooting these young women, I had a behind-the-scenes view, where I could see that they weren't actually happy. They were incredibly hard on themselves, being compared and critiqued for their outward appearance, the extreme dieting and workouts, as well as drugs and eating disorders, which often stemmed from the need to maintain very low body weights. And there was such an incredible lack of representation of women of color as well, so we were all being held to this exceedingly unattainable beauty ideal.

Because of my weight, wherever I went people wanted to talk to me about health. Yet no one wanted to address the mental health of the women who were adversely affected by the saturation of messages assaulting their psyche on a daily basis, which said "you do not stack up." I wanted to be a part of that conversation because I wanted to empower women.

Why did you start *Volup2*?

I felt that there was no magazine within the plus-size world that was strongly editorial. You would never see that edgy sexiness that French *Vogue* has. I also felt that a lot of different types of people were forgotten by fashion, so I didn't want a plus-exclusive magazine. It seems plus sizes are still excluded from mainstream fashion magazines beyond a token gesture annually in a Body issue or "Love

Yourself"–type issue, but for the most part we don't exist. So that is why we make our own publications. While I do shoot some agency models, I also will include people who have never modeled in their life. I include people size twenty-six and up, of all different body shapes. For me it's about genuine diversity.

Why is showing disabled people and different ethnicities and ages an important part of your content?

Fashion is consumed by the masses, so why on earth do we make a choice of exclusion over celebrating the diversity of humanity?

People who live with cancer exist, people who are amputees or wheelchair-bound exist, transgender people exist, women actually do exist after the age of twenty-five, small people exist, burn survivors, and people with genetic differences exist. There are around seventy-five different ethnic groups in the world (according to the CIA), so why is the fashion industry showcasing nearly 80 percent white people? It isn't only unjust, it is astonishingly boring. Yes, beauty ethics have traditionally been aspirational, but we evolve as a society and we can change the dynamic to celebrating each person's individual beauty.

> FASHION IS CONSUMED BY THE MASSES, SO WHY ON EARTH DO WE MAKE A CHOICE OF EXCLUSION OVER CELEBRATING THE DIVERSITY OF HUMANITY?

What have been some of your favorite campaigns that you've created?

I love the images of burn survivors I shot for a hat story. I love my work with Harnaam Kaur. She is a bearded lady from the UK whose story went viral after talking about her struggle with polycystic ovary syndrome. I enjoyed thinking about what I would choose to have as hair were it not to exist, when I shot a model with alopecia. Shooting a model with vitiligo made me think a lot about skin color and prejudice. It is frustrating to me to be continually putting out original content that challenges the norm, and it goes utterly unnoticed, yet some mainstream magazine/brand may include the occasional commercial beauty with some curves, and they are lauded as revolutionary. Insert eye-roll.

Where do you hope to see yourself, and the fashion industry, in ten years?

In ten years, I hope I'll be rocking big gray hair and following none of the rules. My hope is that the fashion industry will be unified in a sense of global celebration of the true spirit of fashion—nonconformity and diversity.

What makes you a powerful woman?

What makes me a powerful woman is my quest to support others.

NEXT–GENERATION
WOMEN

AS A YOUNG WOMAN GROWING UP, I WISH SOMEONE HAD told me that I had the potential to change the world and that I didn't have to wait until I was an adult to do great things. Yet here I am today in my thirties, a mom of two, creating spaces for more young women to be seen, heard, and aspired-to. This feels like the place I was meant to land—a place that says to all the younger women, girls, and femmes out there that they have what it takes to do something great.

It's worth taking a look at how Millennials and Gen Z are shaping the world today and how they are having an impact on the fight for gender equality. A recent US Census Bureau analysis shows that as more young women obtained college degrees, delayed having children, and joined the workforce, they edged out Millennial men for better-paying jobs.

While Gen Z, often referred to as "iGen" for being born into a tech-driven world, have only just begun to enter the workforce, their impact on the US economy and culture is already undeniable. By 2020, Generation Z will account for 40 percent of all consumers in the United States, and they are expected to make up 30 percent of the labor force by 2030. They are the most diverse generation in history, and up to 60 percent of Gen Z-ers say they want their jobs to impact the world—and it looks like they are well on their way to doing this.

ALEXA CARLIN

ALEXA CARLIN IS A TRUE MILLENNIAL ROCK STAR AND INSPIRATION FOR YOUNG WOMEN EVERYWHERE. AS SOMEONE WHO WAS LITERALLY ON THE VERGE OF DEATH, ALEXA REMINDS US ALL THAT WE NEED TO LIVE EVERY DAY TO THE MAX IN ORDER TO FULFILL OUR POTENTIAL. HAVING BEEN GIVEN A SECOND CHANCE AT LIFE, SHE IS WASTING NO TIME IN USING HER PLATFORM AND PASSION TO SEE OTHER YOUNG WOMEN LIKE HER LIVE EMPOWERED LIVES. THROUGH HER SPEAKING, CONFERENCES, AND HER SOCIAL MEDIA PRESENCE, SHE EMBODIES THE SPIRIT OF WHAT *TODAY'S WONDER WOMEN* IS ALL ABOUT.

LIFE TAKES YOU ON CRAZY ADVENTURES, FROM THE most fun experiences to turns that you never thought you would experience. Flashback to January 26, 2013, a day for celebration, the long-anticipated event to celebrate the success of *Hello Perfect*, an inspirational blog I founded while in college to help instill confidence in young girls and women. Instead, my mom, who was in town for the celebration, rushed me to the hospital and my life changed forever. Looking back, this journey served as the catalyst that propelled me to become the leader I am today. Triumph over tragedy, turning obstacles into opportunities.

It was that day back in 2013 that I went from living on top of the world only months away from college graduation to being induced into a medical coma and given a 1 percent chance of living. A few hours before the *Hello Perfect* celebration was about to start, I was not feeling well and it was getting hard for me to breathe. My mom knew something was wrong and rushed me to the emergency room, where a few hours later the doctors were telling her to call my family, as I only had twenty-four hours left to live.

My body went into septic shock and it was at this moment my life changed forever. I was in a coma for six days and in the intensive care unit for a total of ten days, and during this time I truly discovered how powerful our minds are.

When I was out of the coma I wasn't able to control anything on my own—I couldn't breathe, move, or speak on my own—but I was aware of my own thoughts. So, during this time, as I was suffering from severe pain with a tube down my throat and hooked up to nine different bags of antibiotics, one entering through my neck, I pictured my mind to be this healthy pink color. I would envision my mind so healthy and then move this healing pink color down to the rest of my body, which, to me, looked like it was black and rotting away as sepsis was killing all of my organs. I did this hour by hour, day in and day out, until I was discharged from the hospital.

This experience alone always reminds me to focus on the things we do have control over. At that moment, I only could control my own thoughts and it is what helped me survive. Whether or not you believe in the spirituality aspect of it, just redirecting my thoughts to something more positive than the pain itself helped me push through. It's so important in business and in life to be conscious of where you choose to direct your energy. The more time you spend on thinking about your current challenges or obstacles, the less energy you have to pursue what you love.

I wish I could say my life has been uphill since this near-death experience, but that's not how life works. A few months after being discharged from the hospital, I was diagnosed with the autoimmune disease ulcerative colitis. If I thought sepsis was a challenge, I had no idea what I was in for. This autoimmune disease has by far been the hardest thing I've ever had to deal with. It's chronic, so I live with it day in and day out. Some days I feel great while other days I have to cancel all of my meetings.

IT'S SO IMPORTANT IN BUSINESS AND IN LIFE TO BE CONSCIOUS OF WHERE YOU CHOOSE TO DIRECT YOUR ENERGY.

After I was diagnosed it was three years of spending my days in and out of the hospital and doctor appointments and for a long time I felt victimized and questioned why, at twenty-one years old, this had to happen to me. I felt like all of my dreams were just taken from me. But while I was going through this health journey, I still was that passionate go-getter I was when I started my first business at seventeen years old. And so I knew that if I wanted to change my life I couldn't wait for things to change; I had to change them myself. It wasn't until I stopped asking myself, "Why did this happen to me?" and began asking myself, "Why did this happen *for* me?" that everything shifted.

Allowing my story to become public was a must. I instinctively knew that sharing my story would help other people. You could say it was a calling because my survival was nothing short of a miracle. I couldn't stay silent. I had to share my journey of turning obstacles into positive energy with the world. After writing and publishing a gluten-free and vegan cookbook in 2014, I started the live-stream show *Morning Motivation with Alexa.* It was here that I began sharing my story, being completely vulnerable and authentic, on a broader platform. I reached audiences around the world, through public speaking engagements and on social media. The great response I received sparked the idea for the next chapter, the Women Empower Expo (WEX). While speaking, I noticed a disconnect with women within communities around the country and that sparked the idea to bring us together. I felt that in order to create real change in your own life, business, and community, people, specifically women, need to connect and collaborate.

As women, it's important to understand that we need to support and empower one another, to grow together and not isolate or put each other down. Once you realize there is enough success for all of us to be successful, the game changes. I think many women, or really people in general, are afraid of pursuing what they love because of the competition, but when you are your authentic self, you have no competition.

In 2016, I launched the first Women Empower Expo in Ft. Lauderdale, Florida. WEX was founded on the values of collaboration over competition. In November 2018 we hosted our third annual WEX conference in South Florida, and we have also added multiple new cities to the event, including Washington, DC. It is an all-day conference, inviting women of all ages and backgrounds to come together to learn from each other. Whether it be digital marketing, funding for your business, or leading the way to get more women in C-suite positions, guests can curate their own sessions and explore unique activations customizing the WEX Experience to meet their personal passions, businesses, and interests.

In addition to hosting these yearly conferences, I spend much of my time traveling around the United States speaking at companies, universities, and conferences, sharing my story to empower others to gain the courage and confidence to pursue their dreams. Public speaking has been the number one marketing vehicle to grow my business and create an impact on thousands of lives. I used to be an extremely shy person, always afraid of speaking up or sharing my opinion, but after I started my first company at seventeen I realized this was what was holding me back from growing my venture.

Many people ask how I went from that shy girl to who I am today. The answer: hard work and practice. Confidence is a skill, which means you can learn and gain it throughout your journey. You just need the belief in yourself and the support behind you to take it to the next level. Since I started speaking professionally in 2014, I have given a TEDx Talk and have been invited by Fortune 500 companies such as Office Depot and Taco Bell to share my journey and help motivate and inspire others to live their best life and follow their dreams. I love meeting, speaking, and listening to women share their goals with me. I always tell people that being able to speak your goals out loud is the first step to making them a reality. We all have superpowers within us; we just need to learn to unearth them from inside and nourish them to blossom.

JACQUELINE MEANS

JACQUELINE MEANS IS THE LIVING EMBODIMENT OF what it looks like to be a next-generation change-maker. She hails from Southbridge, Wilmington, in Delaware, often referred to as "Murdertown USA," where shootings and robberies are the norm. It is also a place where more than 60 percent of kids drop out of school, making it a city that has one of the highest dropout rates in the country. Jackie has defied these odds. She is a hard-working student who attends the Delaware Military Academy, where she maintains a 4.0 GPA. Jackie is only fifteen years old, and because of her passion for science, technology, engineering, and math, she founded a program to empower other girls—Wilmington Urban STEM Initiative.

Tell me about your upbringing in Southbridge, Wilmington, and what you witnessed in your community.

Where I live I often hear gunshots from my home and have even witnessed someone get shot right across the street from my home. But I am doing my part to change the stigma associated with Southbridge. We all care about this community and know we are better than this stigma.

How difficult was it for you to see so many kids take a different path?

Seeing other kids my age take a path so drastically different from my own, becoming part of gangs or falling victim to violence and

Jacqueline Means (left)

drug addiction, is hard. Knowing that if they only had the resources available to them, they could be so much more than the stereotypes surrounding them is difficult. That is part of the reason why I started my initiative: so I could provide a different picture of what life could be to those who were only getting one image of their potential future.

Where did your passion for STEM come from?

Ever since I was little, I can remember being absolutely obsessed with chemical reactions, like baking soda and vinegar or Mentos and soda, and just loving all things science-y and STEM related.

Tell me about the program you started and how many girls you have impacted so far.

Wilmington Urban STEM Initiative is an initiative I started that is dedicated to bringing science, technology, engineering, and mathematics to the underprivileged girls of Wilmington. I have improved the lives of the girls who attend my events by giving them a newfound love for STEM. Having STEM skills is necessary to thrive in the twenty-first century, making it imperative that today's youth are capable and prepared to live in the inevitable STEM-forward future.

My goal is to change the girls' negative mind-set about STEM, which I feel I have accomplished, because, from when they walk in to when they leave, they go from, "This stinks! We have to do science and math stuff!" to, "That was so fun! Science is actually really cool!" Through my Girls Empowerment STEM Events, I've been able to positively impact over 350 young girls and counting. I am showing the girls that they can overcome negative stereotypes and dominate STEM fields where we remain underrepresented.

At each event, every girl not only gets to do her own science experiments (including making ice cream), they also get to see an interactive antibullying demonstration, and an inspiring talk from prominent women from their community, including Congresswoman Lisa Blunt-Rochester and Lieutenant Governor Bethany Hall Long.

> WITH SO MANY NEGATIVE INFLUENCES ON SOCIAL MEDIA AND IN SOCIETY, I THINK IT'S IMPORTANT FOR YOUNG GIRLS, ESPECIALLY GIRLS OF COLOR, TO SEE A POSITIVE, BLACK, FEMALE ROLE MODEL TO LOOK UP TO AND ASPIRE TO BE LIKE.

Lisa Blunt-Rochester is the first black woman to represent Delaware in Congress, and she also won her re-election. What does it mean to the young girls in your program to see a successful and powerful black woman standing in front of them?

With so many negative influences on social media and in society, I think it's important for young girls, especially girls of color, to see a positive, black, female role model to look up to and aspire to be like. By having someone as important and powerful as the

Congresswoman come to my event, they are being shown that they always have someone in their corner, rooting for them to succeed and overcome any obstacles and/or challenges they may face in their lives.

She too has faced a lot of adversity, but she didn't let that stop her. She speaks to the girls about her adversity and how they just have to persevere through it to accomplish your goals in life.

How would you encourage other leaders in towns where there are many kids dropping out and a lack of resources, especially for young girls?

I would encourage them to think of the impact they could have on those young girls' lives. I'd tell them that they can do absolutely anything they put their mind to. And that as long as they work hard and stay true to their values, they can do anything. I'd tell them to start in their own school or local community center.

Who are your heroes in life, and why?

I just love Dr. Teri Quinn-Grey. She is a chemist for the DuPont Company and a wonderful person. She was a speaker at one of my first Girls Empowerment STEM Events, and she spoke about the importance and power of believing in one's own abilities. As a black woman in America, her odds of being successful in the STEM field were not high, but she defied those odds and changed her circumstances for the betterment of everyone.

Finally, what makes you a powerful woman?

My resolve to be successful and my determination to be unstoppable, not stopping when you fail. Failure is a necessary step in every journey, and to be unstoppable means to know that it's okay to get discouraged, and it's okay to take a step back, but it's never okay to walk away, and I never walk away from a challenge. I believe that is what makes me a powerful young woman.

MENA & ZENA NASIRI

SISTERS MENA AND ZENA NASIRI, FROM ROCHESTER, Michigan, are the creators of a nonprofit organization called Girls of the Crescent, which addresses the need for more representation of Muslim girls and women in the media. Specifically, Mena and Zena were concerned that as young Muslim women, they were not seeing enough nuanced and varied narratives in books and media that featured positive representations of Muslim women and girls, so they decided to do something about it.

The ultimate goal is to make sure that children like them will be able to read books with characters like themselves and to increase diversity in literature.

How did the idea for Girls of the Crescent come about, and what does the name mean?

MENA NASIRI: In fourth grade, we were given a school project: to research a person who we looked up to. We both went to our public library with female Muslim women in mind that were huge role models to us and we couldn't find any books about them. Later we began to realize the same thing occurred in other genres, that there was a shortage of books about Muslim girls.

ZENA NASIRI: The name Girls of the Crescent comes from the crescent moon being the symbol of Islam and us being girls helping other girls.

As avid readers, what kind of books do you both love the most?

ZENA: I love all types of books, from autobiographies to fantasy adventure novels, but I tend to mostly read young adult romance novels. My favorite are books that also focus on outside issues, one of those books being *The Lines We Cross* by Randa Abdel-Fattah. It's about a female Muslim teenager who immigrated to Australia as a refugee. She had to face lots of anti-immigration sentiment while also juggling school and it incorporates lots of teen romance.

Zena and Mena Nasiri (left to right)

MENA: I have found myself enjoying a lot of books assigned in school, from *The House of the Scorpion* to *The Curious Incident of the Dog in the Night-time*, which are both about a unique character trying to fit in with the rest of the world. My all-time-favorite book is *The Lines We Cross*, like my sister said. I think a big part of it was reading about a character with my name and it was really enjoyable and eye-opening to read about someone so similar to me.

How do you think books can play a role in shaping our perceptions of the world and the people around us?

MENA: A lot of people are not exposed to diversity in their communities and schools, and books with representation can provide that exposure. Books with Muslim characters can be focused more on religious aspects or simply include a character who is Muslim. Either way, these books are able to shape people's perspectives of society by showcasing diversity and providing a new point of view. Also these books can mean so much for Muslim kids themselves, by providing them with a sense of acceptance and inclusion in the world that they may not see portrayed in the media or in their communities.

How are you working with libraries and schools to help them diversify their collections?

ZENA: We have donated books from our list to libraries and school and we've also seen that many of them have used our list as a reference to add books to their collection themselves. So far we have collected and donated over three hundred books to various schools and libraries around our community. We've also had many librarians tell us that our project has inspired them to diversify their libraries by adding books featuring many different cultures, ethnicities, races, and religions.

> WE HOPE THAT BY INCREASING DIVERSE BOOKS AND BY SPREADING POSITIVE MESSAGES ABOUT MUSLIM GIRLS, WE CAN CREATE A MORE ACCEPTING AND RESPECTFUL COMMUNITY.

How can an organization like yours work to dismantle harmful ideas and promote inclusiveness?

MENA: There are a lot of biases and stereotypes centered around Muslims that are portrayed in the media and throughout our world today. Both my sister and I have personally experienced ignorance and hate because of our identities and we hope that by increasing diverse books and by spreading positive messages about Muslim girls, we can create a more accepting and respectful community.

What makes you both powerful women?

MENA: I think that I am my own strongest advocate and the fact that I am so passionate about what I'm doing makes me excited and ready to impact people. I love being able to tell people that I am a Muslim woman, that I have also started a nonprofit and accomplished many things. It is a great feeling to prove common stereotypes wrong and show people what Muslims and women can do.

ZENA: I have faced many obstacles in my life, from just being a Muslim woman to being a teenager running a nonprofit. I'm proud to be able to say that I have impacted people, and knowing that girls like me will feel empowered and strong because of my actions helps me keep going. I think that any woman is powerful if she is able to put her mind to something and do what she loves.

ESTEFANI ALARCON

MEET ESTEFANI ALARCON, A YOUNG WOMAN FROM Los Angeles who is using her voice and her passion to give more visibility to young Latinas like her in media and journalism. She graduated from Mount Saint Mary's University with a dual degree in film, media, and social justice and journalism and new media, and is now a graduate student at New York University. Estefani is taking her experience as a young Latina growing up in South Los Angeles and creating spaces for more people of color, especially women of color in the diaspora of Southern California, to share their stories with the world. Along with her focus on immigration and incarceration, which she has written about, Estefani is also the founder of an online newspaper called *Dear Southside*, which is focused on telling the untold stories of South Los Angeles.

Tell us about growing up in South Central Los Angeles and how it shaped your perspective on the world and people.

Growing up in South Central was what I needed as a young immigrant coming from El Salvador. I felt welcomed, supported, and safe. Everyone around me was working hard. As an immigrant you build with the only resources you have, which are often little to none, and the people in my community didn't have a lot. That really motivated me.

I lived in South Central and went to school in midcity so at a young age I was riding the bus, and getting home from school late. The people I rode the bus with were also commuting further out to clean houses, take care of someone's kids, and get to their job. I learned so much on those buses, met so many people, and it all built a strong bond between South Central and me. Every stop from Jefferson to Manchester introduced me to someone new, something new. It made me grow a profound love for my community, the food, the culture, but most importantly the people.

As a young girl, what drew you to become interested in media and journalism? Did you have any role models or heroes?

I grew up watching telenovelas and the evening news with my family. It was something we did together while eating dinner. I could never identify with any of the characters, but I loved how it brought us together and developed a deeper dialogue about politics, identity, race, and more. But my family's stories drew me into media and journalism; I want to tell their stories. I love hearing them, I love gathering together and watching my mom impersonate the people she is telling the story about. I believe I am a storyteller because of my mother and father.

One of my favorite actresses growing up was America Ferrera. Her character in *The Sisterhood of the Traveling Pants* was the first introduction I had to a Latina character that was fuller-figured in

American film. I also loved the news anchor Ilia Calderon on *Noticiero Univision*; she was the first Afro-Latina I had ever seen anchoring on a Latinx news platform. For a long time, I wanted to be a news anchor but didn't see it as possible because of the lack of inclusivity in the broadcast journalism when it comes to image.

You are currently studying at NYU and also working for the Geena Davis Institute on Gender in Media. What are some of the ways the GDIGM is impacting film and TV culture at large, that people may not know about?

SOUTH CENTRAL
IS MORE THAN
WHAT IT HAS
PREVIOUSLY
BEEN PAINTED AS.
THERE ARE SO
MANY PEOPLE
DOING GREAT WORK.
I WANT TO
HIGHLIGHT THEM.

Women, people of color, the LGBTQ community, and people with disabilities all have been underrepresented in the media. The Geena Davis Institute is amplifying those people through data that shows that by representing everyone there are better results not only through the box office but also in how women see themselves.

One of their studies looked at how much screen time women get even if they are the lead in the film and the results were that 77 percent of the screen time is men even though women make up 51.9 percent of the population. Their work is incredibly important because providing production companies with this research would be a catalyst for change. Men, especially white men, are not the only ones who walk this world. We need to represent every community because it matters.

Who are some Latinx people that are currently inspiring you with their visibility and voice?

I'm currently inspired by Indigenous actress Yalitza Aparicio. Her role in *Roma* felt very personal; I saw my mom in her role. I saw all the black and brown women raising other people's children missing out on their own children's growth to provide for them in her role. I saw my grandparents' home in that car driveway. Not often do we see a brown indigenous woman on screen speaking in her native tongue and Spanish. Hollywood loves white Latinx actors and actresses, but that doesn't represent Latinx culture as a whole. Yalitza's success gives me hope for other Indigenous women like her.

You are the founder of a newspaper called *Dear Southside*. What made you want to create this?

One day my friends and I were leaving Downtown Los Angeles. One of my friends, who is now the editor of *Dear Southside*, had written a few pieces for *LA Downtowner*, so after picking up an issue, I told my friends "this is so cool, I wish we had this in South Central." That sparked the idea. I felt our stories are never told from our own perspective. Whenever I hear about South Central in the media it's never good. I want to change that narrative because South Central is more than what it has previously been painted as. There are so many people doing great work. I want to highlight them.

I was also noticing my community slowly changing, people moving in and longtime residents moving out. I wanted to encourage people to not "leave the hood," but to support local businesses and help them sustain each other. I focus on businesses, nonprofits, people, and anything that shares the real essence of South Central.

You have also written articles for a number of publications, including *Teen Vogue* and *Rewire*. How has writing become a source of power for you?

Writing serves more as healing than power for me. It has allowed me to tell my own story, which is such a privilege. In journalism, among other media platforms, we often have others telling our narrative and they don't always get it right. They are just now accepting that they need to diversify their newsrooms to have the stories reflect the audience they are writing for. Through my writing I have been able to educate people about news and policies that affect the immigrant community.

The media loves our stories, they just don't allow us to be the ones to tell them. There's a slight shift in that right now and I think we need to keep pushing and demanding more diverse narratives being told by people of color, most importantly women of color.

What kind of change are you most passionate about seeing in the future, and how do you work toward that?

I want to see more women being bosses. On sets directing, behind the screen shooting, in newsrooms, owning businesses, starting businesses, taking over tech, everything. I want to see women of color take up the space they deserve, I want to see them being acknowledged and recognized for their work. I want them to be compensated for their labor, rightfully. I want to see them with bigger production budgets, trusted and allowed to get shit done, because they can. We need to uplift each other, hire each other, support each other. Victoria Mahoney, a director I consider a role model, once talked about the 100th woman behind us. I think of her often and how I am making room for the 100th woman behind me.

What would you say to other young women, especially women of color, who feel like their voice doesn't matter?

Our voices, our stories, our ideas, our thoughts do matter and are worthy of being heard; if not, there wouldn't be so many people trying to steal it. Tell your story, tell it unapologetically, tell it with your voice, your tone. You will receive no's, and rejection is difficult at first, but then it gets to a point where the no's are just background noise trying to distract us. Keep going.

And finally, what makes you a powerful woman?

What makes me a powerful woman is my will, dedication, and resilience.

JAMIE MARGOLIN

IT IS ARGUED THAT CLIMATE CHANGE IS THE MOST urgent human rights issue of our time. It is no surprise, then, that the most vocal people in the fight and race against the clock are the generation that is going to be the most affected—Generation Z. While world leaders continue to debate over whether they will take action, the youth of today, especially young women, are taking the lead in a powerful way. In the United States, the charge is being led by Jamie Margolin, founder of an organization called Zero Hour. She and her cohorts, including cofounders Nadia Nazar and Madelaine Tew, have inspired students from across the country to protest, walk out, raise awareness, and put pressure on lawmakers at both the state and national level. Jamie's passion reminds me that we have the power to create change, no matter our age, gender, background, or status.

When did you launch Zero Hour and what prompted you to do this?

I founded Zero Hour in the summer of 2017, when I was fifteen. I have been an environmental organizer in my community of Seattle, Washington, for a long time. I was working with local environmental youth-led movements in my hometown, but no matter how much we worked, our politicians, our leaders, companies, and the media paid no attention. There was even an instance when I was trying to help get a

bill passed in the Washington state legislature where the head of the environmental committee's office ignored all my and the other youth's calls and emails asking about the condition of the bill, until they let it die in committee. Ever since the Women's March in 2017 I had a vision of youth all over the world marching and demanding climate action, but I had no idea how to make it happen. So in the summer of 2017, after a huge pattern of climate disasters I finally took the plunge and put a call out on social media that I was organizing a Youth Climate March, and invited youth to join me.

The organization is made up entirely of youth activists, and the majority are women of color. Why is a diverse founding team important to Zero Hour?

We are not diverse simply to say we are diverse. We are a diverse team because that is crucial in properly addressing the roots of the climate crisis. Anyone who is a victim of societal systems of oppression like racism, poverty, and patriarchy are automatically more vulnerable to the effects of climate change. Women of color all around the world are feeling the worst impacts of climate change, and those most impacted by a problem need to be at the forefront of the solutions to it.

How does it make you feel to see other teens around the world marching and protesting about climate change as well?

I feel a part of a big global climate action community, and so much less alone. Back in 2017 when

I started the #ThisIsZeroHour movement it felt like we were alone in terms of youth climate movements in the public eye. This was before Greta Thunberg did her first strike for climate action. Back when I was a scared fifteen-year-old trying to do my part to stop the climate crisis, youth climate activism was hardly known or recognized in the mainstream media. We had no money, no notoriety, and yet the movement we young women of color in the United States started was the first domino that led to the mainstreaming of high school climate justice activism that you know today.

THE VAST MAJORITY OF FOSSIL FUEL PROJECTS AND ENERGY EXTRACTION SITES ARE BUILT IN LOW-INCOME COMMUNITIES, IMMIGRANT COMMUNITIES, AND COMMUNITIES OF COLOR.

With nothing but determination and the Internet, we American girls organized the first-ever Youth Climate March and Youth Climate Lobby Day in Washington, DC, and twenty-five other cities around the world. The day of the Youth Climate March, July 21, 2018, there was a rainstorm in Washington, DC. Everyone was drenched and at one point it looked like our cries for climate justice were drowned in the storm.

But after we dried off from the rain and opened our computers and the Sunday *New York Times*, we realized that our scrappy little protest was the first match that sparked an international movement of youth for climate justice. Even when you're just a teenage girl drenched in a rainstorm and it feels like no one is listening to you, they are. And thankfully we have a massive global community now of climate justice activists making the world wake up to the severity of this issue.

Can you explain the intersectionality between climate change, social justice, and racial justice?

The vast majority of fossil fuel projects and energy extraction sites are built in low-income communities, immigrant communities, and communities of color. Why? Because these people are already victims of the racist system of oppression, and governments and corporations exploit their powerlessness. A 2008 report that reviewed data collected over twenty years found that more than half of the people living within two miles of toxic waste facilities in the United States are people of color. In the aftermath of climate disasters, such as extreme weather conditions, efforts to rebuild communities of color and low-income communities are often inadequate compared to efforts to rebuild higher-income and white communities. The most powerful example of this inequity was seen in the black community of New Orleans after Hurricane Katrina. Black homeowners received eight thousand dollars less per family in government aid than white homeowners due to disparities in housing values. None of these examples are a coincidence.

Because people of color and immigrants are already victims of racism, they are more vulnerable to corporations targeting them. Fossil fuel and big agriculture corporations like Shell or Monsanto need there to be as little pushback as possible on the projects they undertake. And because wealthy white citizens have the money, the power, and our current system on their side, corporations would not be able to get away with building toxic chemical or extraction plants in those wealthy neighborhoods. Take, for example, the Dakota Access Pipeline: a fossil fuel pipeline designed to transport up to half a million barrels of crude oil daily from North Dakota to Illinois. According to ABC News, the construction of the pipeline was originally going to be built through a majority white, nonindigenous community, but when that community rejected it in the interests of protecting their water and health of their citizens, it was rerouted to instead be built on indigenous land. And even though there was large pushback against the construction of the pipeline on this indigenous land, their outcry (while it gained a lot of media attention) was ultimately not respected and the pipeline was built anyway.

Why do you think it is important for women to be front and center leading the movement for climate action?

Because we bear the biggest burden for the climate crisis. Figures from the UN Gateway on Gender Equality and Empowerment of women indicate that 80 percent of people displaced by climate change are women. Roles as primary caregivers and providers of food and fuel make them more vulnerable when flooding and drought occur. According to the BBC, in central Africa, where up to 90 percent of Lake Chad has disappeared, nomadic indigenous groups are particularly at risk. As the lake's shoreline recedes, women have to walk much further to collect water. In the dry season, men go to the towns, leaving women to look after the community. With dry seasons now becoming longer, women are working harder to feed and care for their families without support—that's an example of the climate crisis disproportionately affecting women where women have the burden of dealing with the effects of the crisis.

Who are some other youth climate activists who are inspiring you right now?

Jasilyn Charger and Tokata Iron Eyes are my biggest inspirations, and they are also friends of mine. They are two amazing young indigenous women who were part of founding the Standing Rock #NODAPL movement. They are such brave water protectors and also amazing friends. Their strength and resilience in the face of everything they are up against reminds me to keep fighting for mother earth.

How can everyday people make change in their own lives to reduce carbon emissions?

Some of the best things you can do to reduce your carbon emissions is eat less meat, travel on airplanes less, eat locally grown food, and use public transit.

Finally, what makes you a powerful woman?

My refusal to apologize for who I am. I am unapologetically female, unapologetically lesbian, unapologetically Latina, and unapologetic in the way that I lead and take up space. People often tell me I need to be quieter, less intense, less queer (I get told to "focus on just the environment" and to "tone down the gay stuff" a lot), and take up less space. But no one is going to hand someone like me a seat at the table. I have to wrestle for it myself, so that's exactly what I do. I own my marginalized identities proudly and go through the world refusing to apologize for who I am.

KENDALL CIESEMIER

KENDALL CIESEMIER IS A NEW YORK–BASED CHICAGO native who has created some incredible achievements in her life so far, but what truly makes Kendall unique is the WHY behind what she does. Her motivation isn't just for self-empowerment, although that is important. Her reason is to help others find their power.

Kendall is a journalist, producer, and entrepreneur who started a nonprofit at the age of eleven to provide for kids in Africa most affected by the AIDS epidemic. During her college years at Georgetown University she created a female empowerment event called the OWN IT Summit, a national women's leadership initiative that helps young women connect with established female leaders in a variety of industries and establish mentoring opportunities. As a journalist and producer Kendall has done some important reporting for platforms such as Mic, The New York Times, and CBS News. She has also been very candid about her own personal health journey, undergoing multiple surgeries for a disease she was born with. Whether she is speaking, sharing stories via her reporting, or appearing on major media outlets about her work, Kendall is adamant about using her social capital for the benefit of others.

Tell us about starting Kids Caring 4 Kids at the age of eleven, and what prompted you to do this.

I first became aware of the AIDS epidemic and its impact in sub-Saharan Africa by watching a TV special. I began to imagine myself living in a mud hut, caring for my younger siblings and grieving the death of my parents, just like I saw happening on TV. Having experienced struggles in my own life, their pain resonated with me and I was in awe of their unwavering hope. That night, I knew I had seen the opportunity I was waiting for—my chance to give my life more purpose than the chronic liver disease I had grown up fighting against.

I realized my purpose in founding Kids Caring 4 Kids, a nonprofit organization that works to inspire and empower young people to help provide basic human needs to children living in sub-Saharan Africa. As I underwent two liver transplants in the summer of 2004, I started by asking well-wishers to donate money, in lieu of gifts and flowers, to help me support the village of Musele, Zambia, the area most highly affected by the AIDS epidemic at the time.

Since then, through Kids Caring 4 Kids, ten thousand young people across the country have banded together to raise over one million dollars. We've helped eight thousand individuals in five countries in Africa through building a high school, dormitories, orphan care centers, a clinic, classrooms, and computer labs, and providing specially built bikes, indoor plumbing, healthy meals, and clean water.

While in college at Georgetown University, you cofounded the OWN IT women's leadership conference. What is the mission behind this annual event?

I started OWN IT with one of my best friends at Georgetown. We held the inaugural summit in April of 2014 and the success of that event spurred national expansion and independence for OWN IT. Our mission is to bridge the gap between female leaders of the twenty-first century and the millennials who admire them, and address the leadership gap. Women have filled the education gap. In fact, women are graduating college at higher rates than men. However, there is still a dearth of women sitting on corporate boards, in science and technology, in C-suite positions, representing us in government, and in other types of leadership roles. Women aren't a monolith AND we are more than 50 percent of the population, so we should have representation everywhere because all industries impact us. OWN IT seeks to provide young women with an opportunity not just to see, but to learn from and connect with women who are living out leadership in a variety of fields

and positions. Similarly, OWN IT seeks to provide well-established women leaders with an outlet to give back and share what they have learned.

One of your most notable reports was for Mic, interviewing Alice Marie Johnson, a woman serving a life without parole sentence for a first-time nonviolent drug offense. Your story captured the attention of Kim Kardashian West, who joined the fight and met with President Trump to ask him for clemency. What was that like for you as a reporter to see one of your stories make such a drastic impact on the life of this woman?

It was such a meaningful thing to witness a story I produced to actually be able to change someone's life, and for Alice, in the end, to be granted clemency after our story. The impact I see is a ripple effect: Alice's life, Kim's life, and all the people Kim has gone on to help. It was so impactful to be on the ground when Alice received clemency, to witness that. Watching Alice walk across the street and see her family across from the prison was pretty powerful. I think, as a journalist, you're taught to just do your job—but you're also a human being. As a journalist, you always dream of your stories having impact and inspiring other people to rethink the world.

AS A JOURNALIST, YOU ALWAYS DREAM OF YOUR STORIES HAVING IMPACT AND INSPIRING OTHER PEOPLE TO RETHINK THE WORLD.

What advice would you give to other young women who aspire to create change but don't know where to begin?

Pay attention to what makes you angry. Channel that anger into change by starting with one little thing. That little thing will undoubtedly grow into a bigger thing—it's a snowball effect. Just jump in.

Finally, what makes you a powerful woman?

I'm a powerful woman because I find my power through being powerful for other people.

WOMEN AND THEIR
ORGANIZATIONS

Raofa Ahrary, *Afghani who worked on first women's magazine in her country*

Anna Akana, *creator of YouTube Red's Youth and Consequences*

Estefani Alarcon, *Latina writer and college student working on behalf of her community*

Angelina Aspuac, *indigenous Guatemalan activist*

Violeta Ayala, *indigenous Bolivian documentary filmmaker*

Cassandra Bankson, *YouTube influencer challenging health and beauty standards*

Alexa Carlin, *founder of Women's Empowerment Expo*

Indira Cesarine, *owner of Untitled Space Gallery highlighting all female artists*

Kendall Ciesemier, *activist for disabled/ journalist for The New York Times*

Sara Cunningham, *founder of Free Mom Hugs supporting LGBTQ+ community*

Farida D, *Arab feminist writer and university professor/author of Rants of a Rebel Arab Feminist*

Velvet D'Amour, *pioneer superplus-size model and photographer*

Amalie De Alwis, *British engineer heading up Code First: Girls*

Laverne Delgado, *program director of Fashion and Freedom helping sex trafficking survivors through fashion*

Gloria Feldt, *founder of Women in Leadership/ former CEO of Planned Parenthood*

Ana Flores, *founder of We All Grow Latina Network, largest digital network of Latina influencers in United States*

Ndumie Funda, *South African LGBTQ activist*

Dorothy Gibbons, *founder of The Rose (breast health clinic)*

Maytal Gilboa, *creator of Emet Comics*

Haben Girma, *disability rights lawyer/first deafblind Harvard Law School Graduate*

Arissa Hall, *project director of National Bail Out*

Mariah Hanson, *founder of "The Dinah," the largest lesbian music festival in the world*

Mia Ives-Rublee, *activist and founder of the Women's March Disability Caucus*

Maya Jafer, *transgender Indian woman/ actress/activist featured in documentary film From Mohammed to Maya*

Betty Lamarr, *founder of EmpowHer Institute helping low income black girls stay on educational track*

Jackie Lomax, *founder of Girls4Science*

Jamie Margolin, *founder of Zero Hour, a US youth-based climate change organization*

Destri Martino, *founder of The Director List, the only comprehensive database of women directors*

Jacqueline Means, *student who started STEM club in Delaware*

Umaimah Mendhro, *founder of VIDA, an online store selling artisanal goods made by people in Pakistan*

Sarah Moshman, *Emmy Award–winning documentary filmmaker of Losing Sight of Shore*

Yasmine Mustafa, *entrepreneur who creates wearable tech products to keep women safe*

Mena and Zena Nasiri, *students who launched Girls of the Crescent, an organization highlighting literature for girls*

Kayla Nguyen, *Lemelson MIT Prize Winner*

Niloufar Nourbakhsh, *composer and pianist who founded Iranian Women's Composers Association*

Jannica Olin, *Swedish actress and activist who started social media campaign to fight stigma of alopecia*

Kedma Ough, *domestic abuse survivor/ motivational speaker/entrepreneur supporting marginalized communities*

Dannielle Owens-Reid, *nonbinary talent manager/cofounder of Everyone Is Gay YouTube channel*

Sage Paul, *founder of Indigenous Fashion Week in Toronto, Canada*

Sahar Paz, *escaped Iran as a girl and launched Own Your Voice Summit*

Mary Pryor, *cofounder of Cannaclusive, a media company breaking stigma of cannabis, especially in communities of color*

Adisyn Pyles and Jiayi, *founders of Freeleaf, an accessories company helping women get out of sex trafficking and prostitution in Asia*

Fraidy Reiss, *founder of Unchained at Last, working to end child marriage in the United States*

Christin Rose, *photographer who launched "She Plays, We Win" campaign highlighting girls in male-dominated sports*

Catherine Schrieber, *Tony– and Olivier– winning Broadway producer/first woman to win Global Producer of the Year award (The Scottsboro Boys, Next Fall)*

Suzanne Siemens and Madeleine Shaw, *founders of Lunapads (reusable feminine products)*

Suzanne Singer, *Native American scientist helping indigenous youth discover STEM*

Shira Tarantino, *advocate for gun control/ founder of ENOUGH campaign*

Shira Taylor, *founder of SEXT, organization that teaches sex education through theater*

Chef Alina Z, *Russian immigrant chef to the stars*

PHOTO CREDITS

ACKNOWLEDGMENTS

THIS BOOK WOULDN'T HAVE BEEN POSSIBLE WITHOUT the help of my own personal wonder women and other superheroes who made it happen!

To my literary agent, Gary Krebs, for finding my blog and taking an interest in the work I am doing around women's stories. Thank you for believing in me and allowing me to tap into an aspect of my creative repertoire I had no idea existed! *Today's Wonder Women* would not exist without you, and I am thrilled to be on this journey with you.

To Fiona Hallowell who believed in the idea from the beginning and championed it. I am forever grateful for your guidance in helping me become a published author! To know there are women like you who understand the power of women's voices and stories in the literary world is encouraging and exciting.

To my parents, Kamni and Dinesh. Thank you for raising me to know I am strong and capable of being the hero of my own story. Thank you for helping me to appreciate the power of our own story through your love of music and art films. Although we are far apart geographically, I always hold you and our family close to my heart and am so blessed to have your support.

To Angelo, Frankie and Zoie. I sometimes have to pinch myself and remember how lucky I am to have such a beautiful family of my own! I cannot call myself "supermom" by any means, but all that matters is that I am your mom, Frankie and Zoie, and am incredibly lucky to have the privilege to raise you with your superdad (Angelo). This book is for you, and I hope I can make you proud with its stories. May it serve as an inspiration for how you live and how your own stories are shared in the future.

To my friend and neighbor Carol Shih. You were the first person I told about Today's Wonder Women, and you have been a constant champion of this project and my ability to make it happen, even at times when I didn't. I am a true believer in the saying "You become a product of the people you surround yourself with," and your friendship has been so encouraging to me. You are a superwoman in your own right and inspire me. May all women and girls have friends like you in their lives.

To the tribe of badass women I get to regularly draw strength from here in Los Angeles at the Empowerment Circle, who inspire me, challenge me, support me, and light my fire. Thank you for being my source of strength. I wouldn't be where I am in my career or life without you, and I am truly honored to know such incredible wonder women.

I'd also like to acknowledge the legacy of both my maternal and paternal grandmothers, superheroes in their own right. Both women are two-time immigrants who raised multiple kids in countries where they had to start all over again and establish a life for themselves. I am forever grateful to their strength, passed down to me, and their willingness to know that moving away from their homeland meant giving their future granddaughter a better life. They are unfortunately not around to see the fruition of this book, but I know they would be proud.

And, finally, to all the wonder women, young and old, and everyday superheroes around the world. I hope you never stop dreaming, believing, and sharing your stories. Your voice matters, and there are people out in the world who need to hear it. May this book serve as inspiration and motivation for you to know you are the hero you have been waiting for.

ABOUT THE

AUTHOR

ASHA DAHYA IS THE FOUNDER AND EDITOR IN CHIEF OF GirlTalkHQ.com: a daily blog dedicated to sharing the voices and stories of global women. Considered a voice of authority in the female empowerment landscape, Dahya has delivered keynote addresses for UN Women, March for Moms, UCLA, EmpowHer Institute, and Mount Saint Mary's University. She is a writer, TEDx speaker, and producer with over fifteen years of experience and is particularly passionate about women's rights and the representation of women in media. Dahya was born in the United Kingdom, raised in Australia, and lives in Los Angeles with her husband and two children.